THE THERAPY RELATIONSHIP

THE THERAPY RELATIONSHIP

A Special Kind of Friendship

Richard Hallam

Routledge
Taylor & Francis Group
LONDON AND NEW YORK

First published 2015 by Karnac Books Ltd.

Published 2018 by Routledge
2 Park Square, Milton Park, Abingdon, Oxon OX14 4RN
711 Third Avenue, New York, NY 10017, USA

Routledge is an imprint of the Taylor & Francis Group, an informa business

British Library Cataloguing in Publication Data

A C.I.P. for this book is available from the British Library

ISBN-13: 9781782202523 (pbk)

Typeset by Medlar Publishing Solutions Pvt Ltd, India

CONTENTS

ACKNOWLEDGEMENTS

A special thanks to Mike Bender, Gordon Cree, Chris Lee, and Clare Penney for their comments on early versions of the manuscript and for innumerable discussions.

ABOUT THE AUTHOR

Richard Hallam trained as a clinical psychologist and has combined university teaching and research with work in a variety of National Health Service settings. His main areas of interest are adult problems, hearing-related complaints, and case formulation. He has published several books, most recently *Virtual Selves, Real Persons* (CUP, 2009) and *Individual Case Formulation* (Elsevier, 2013). He now works as an independent researcher and in private practice.

PREFACE

As my title implies, a key message running through this book is that a therapist is a special kind of friend. To be more precise, I view friendship as the cultural model for the therapy relationship, despite the fact that friendship and therapy differ in important ways. If my position is credible, it has important implications for how we understand the ethics of the relationship and how therapy fits into the politics and structure of society. One implication, it seems to me, is that the drive to make therapy into an application of science and a technically managed service will encounter strict limits.

In order to be rationalised technically, the process of therapy has to be defined precisely, that is, by using a classification of clients' problems, specifying therapy skills, and agreeing criteria for effectiveness. Like any productive process, the raw materials and products have to be clearly identified. At present, this trick is performed by declaring that there are such things as mental disorders, that they have definable forms, and that they can be alleviated or cured. There are variations on this theme, substituting terms such as emotional distress and well-being, but the underlying assumption remains the same: process and product can be quantified. On the face of it, it is not unreasonable to want to have a measure of what clients have gained from therapy.

The task is not an impossible one but we should not be content with over-simple solutions.

Friendship has been a popular subject for writers throughout recorded history. On close examination, it can be seen that friendship shares many of its essential features with the aims and moral ethos of therapy. By tracing the ancestry of friendship in some of the written sources, my aim is to demystify therapy and write about it in a manner that departs from the styles found in literature on the subject. Broadly speaking, there are three styles. The first, directed at professionals, is full of obscure terminology and must be a turn-off for any lay reader. The second style avoids being pretentious, and aims to present ideas in a clear manner for the informed reader. There are some excellent self-help books in this genre. The third style is found in books that peddle simplistic philosophies, which are often no more than bland common sense; if intended for self-help, the methods are too general to provide specific advice.

I would like my book to fall into the second style but I hope that my attempt to avoid jargon will not be taken to imply that I believe that either friendship or therapy lack mystery and complexity. I also do not mean to suggest that a therapist possesses no more skills or personal qualities than a good friend. Having practised for over forty years, I know that each new client is a challenge who is expecting more than a sympathetic ear. Professionals get paid for what they do and this is also a major departure from friendship. Remuneration is necessary because even friends with the best of intentions have a limited supply of well-meaning concern for others.

My book is directed at two sets of readers. First, there will be those who are not very familiar with the field of psychotherapy. I will be explaining the philosophical, technical, political, and ethical aspects of three different approaches to therapy. This should help the reader to make sense of the huge number of schools of therapy currently competing for attention. They offer their services to people who may be in turmoil about their emotions, their relationships, or their troublesome habits. The people who provide the service regard themselves as professionals and refer to themselves as counsellors, psychoanalysts, psychotherapists, clinical psychologists, and other kindred titles. Members of the public rarely seem to know (or have little interest in finding out) what these different professional titles signify. This is not too surprising because cross-cutting the professions are ways of working that express quite different assumptions and methods. A counsellor, for example, could claim allegiance to any school of therapy. My first aim, then, is to explain differences in approach to readers who are not very familiar with them.

I have grouped the ways of working into three main approaches whose early histories are at least distinct. The early exponents stated their assumptions clearly, and so I use them to highlight distinctions that have now become rather blurred. The founding figures of each approach still have their faithful adherents but, on the whole, in the last forty years there has been a profound muddying of the waters. The field of psychological therapy is in a constant flux of splitting, re-amalgamating, and reinventing itself. It is almost impossible for me to adopt terms that do not favour one approach over another. As a compromise, I have settled on the word "therapist" (or "psychotherapist") to refer to anyone who provides professional help, and "client" to refer to the person on the receiving end. The word "patient" is associated with medicine and psychoanalysis, and it has the connotation (for me) that a person is in a deferential position in relation to the "expert" they are consulting. Most therapists now adopt a collaborative style, encouraging clients to contest, on an equal basis, the advice they receive. I do not want to dispense with the need for expertise, and as long as therapists are completely open about the rationale of the therapy methods they are using, it need not denote an authoritarian approach. In fact, for some therapists, it is now the clients who are the experts (on how to deal with their problem) and this is, of course, a basic premise of self-help.

This book is not intended as a consumer guide to "best buys" in therapy. My aim in describing three approaches is to highlight theoretical foundations, philosophical values, and the rationale for producing change. I cannot hope to provide an overview of therapy methods or "good practice". Any attempt to do so would be a foolhardy undertaking given the enormity of the task.

The question of relative effectiveness is also too complex to deal with in a short book but I do discuss how contemporary researchers go about evaluating the benefits of therapy. The influence of competition is much more evident in psychotherapy than it is in medicine. Each school is keen to prove that its techniques are valuable (and usually more valuable) than the techniques of competitors. In medicine there are clearer criteria for deciding which treatments are more effective or less costly. In the case of therapy, there is little agreement over the criteria that could be applied to decide these questions. Medicine is more closely linked to science and therefore to rules of argument about effectiveness. By contrast, claims for effectiveness amongst schools of therapy seem to be part of a branding exercise in a marketplace of other service providers. In order to substantiate their appeal, they may cite the work of the founding figures of their own movement, some of whom have become cultural icons. One reason for the amount of diversity in contemporary therapy is the pressure to offer something new, promising, and fashionable. Although lip-service is paid to evaluation, the chief rule of the game seems to be to strengthen a brand and maintain difference. There is little sign that the protagonists want to resolve a debate.

The lack of consensus stems from the fact that there is little agreement over how to define the individual and social benefits. In the case of privately funded therapy, consumer choice plays a large part in determining which kinds of therapy survive. For governments, insurance companies, and health management companies, different considerations dictate which services they are willing to resource. Although the buzz words are "cost-effectiveness" and "evidence-based therapy", these concepts disguise a lack of agreement, alluded to earlier, over how therapy can benefit individuals or society. It has been assumed that, as in medicine, there are therapies that can withstand the rigours of research evaluation. I will criticise current attempts to prove therapy's worth, while also acknowledging the complexity of the task. I do happen to believe that "progress" in certain areas is possible, in the sense that the application of psychological and social theory to individual and social problems can be justified by their results.

I will have fulfilled the first aim of my book if the reader has become more aware of what kinds of therapy are on offer, the rationale for offering them, and is more confident in choosing an approach to therapy, if they happen to be seeking it. For other readers, it may help them to make sense of help they were offered in the past.

My second group of readers is likely to be composed of people already working as therapists. I will ask, What sort of activity is therapy? How does it relate to ethics and politics? Should it aim to alleviate distress or is it a form of problem solving? Does effectiveness mean the same thing to different therapists? I will examine some of the key findings in psychotherapy research and call into question the inferences that have been drawn from them. For instance, one key finding is that any kind of *bona fide* therapy is just as likely to produce a successful outcome as any other. In other words, it wouldn't matter greatly whether a person receives psychodynamic therapy, cognitive behavioural therapy, or a medicinal drug. All are said to have a similar outcome for the same identified problem. I will cast doubt on this conclusion. I will also be questioning the reasoning that lies behind an emphasis on "client characteristics" and on the "therapy relationship", which in both cases derives from the findings of research.

Some of the variation in success that individual therapists achieve is attributable to their personal style or skills. I will review this research and question how the different ingredients of therapy might interact, bearing in mind the similarities between therapy and friendship. A therapist might be perceived as an authoritative expert, as an empathic and attentive listener, as an expert in problem-solving, as a coercive agent of the state, as a wise healer, and so on. There are many ways of conceiving the therapy relationship and this is especially obvious in my comparison of the three main approaches to therapy.

In the course of exploring the research literature, I will ask what motivates someone to become a therapist, how the therapy relationship is experienced by clients, and what difficulties typically arise within it. Non-participants in therapy, such as sociologists and political commentators, have also had much to say about the issues I raise, and I will be examining their views. For some critics, therapy necessarily involves an abuse of power. It has been well documented that therapy has been exploitative in the past and probably continues in this way to some extent. For this and other reasons, therapy is carefully regulated. I discuss professional regulation in the light of the similarities between therapy and friendship.

It is perhaps too obvious to state that most people solve problems on their own. I devote a chapter to self-help where this involves at least some participation by a professional helper. Advice is now being disseminated by telephone, video conferencing, texting, and email. Although in this book I restrict myself to professional help, mutual support, in its various forms, is also based on friendship. Readers coming from this background may find points of similarity with a therapist perceived as a "special kind of friend".

CHAPTER ONE

Introduction to the issues

People seek help for different reasons, although a problem often fits into one of the common categories, such as a difficulty in relationships, depressed mood, or anxiety. Help could have been sought from a doctor, a teacher, a family member, a cleric, or a friend. What, then, is different about help from a therapist and what sort of social role does this person fill? There are enough jokes circulating about therapists to be safe in assuming that everyone has some conception of what the job entails. Having worked as a therapist over several decades, it has always been a surprise that people slip into this intimate social relationship with me, a complete stranger, with relative ease. As one client recently said after only a couple of hours' acquaintance, "I have never told that to anyone else before, not even to myself."

The assumption I will be making is that a therapist is perceived as a special kind of friend, and this makes it easy to open up. A therapist is not a doctor who diagnoses your disorder and prescribes a remedy; not a teacher who wants to know what it is you want to learn; not a family member to whom you have obligations, and who stills sees you as a brother, sister, son, or daughter; not a religious advisor, for which role a therapist is seen as unqualified; and, finally, not an ordinary friend. We do of course seek out friends to lend an ear to a personal problem or ask for advice about a moral dilemma. Friends can be a great source of strength and support. However, some problems have to be concealed from friends and even from lifelong intimate partners. A friend's attention span is usually limited. Having listened to you, he is likely to want to pour out one of his own concerns for an equal length of time. A therapist, by contrast, offers many of the advantages of friendship without its encumbrances. Once viewed as a special kind of friend, there need be no protracted "getting to know you" stage because an idea of what to expect has already been established.

A client's readiness to fall into a friendship-like relationship suggests to me that therapy and friendship share deeply embedded cultural rules, and perhaps, also, both are grounded in our biology. The primatologist Frans de Waal (2013) believes that a drive to form friendships can be observed in chimpanzees and bonobos, and also between these animals and humans. Their social behaviour, in addition to signs of "care", seems to include jealousy, revenge, mock fights, and reconciliations. It is likely, then, that the propensity to form friendships has a strong biological as well as a cultural basis, and that, at times, friendship formation can happen very quickly.

The role of a professional therapist is, of course, of recent historical origin. It differs from ordinary friendship because it is the client who is expected to open up while the therapist listens and asks questions. It is non-reciprocal in the sense that the therapist is not seeking help from the client and pays attention in a way that friends rarely do. Aside from these clear differences, therapy shares with friendship most of its norms and virtues: trust, confidentiality, genuineness, commitment, and a disavowal of vested interest. This, at least, is the ideal, and I will later mention circumstances that put these norms under strain. Nevertheless, the ethical standards used to regulate therapy are not far removed from the values that constitute friendship.

Psychotherapy addresses issues both big and small, and these are usually situated in a moral context (Miller, 2004, 2005). We do not expect a psychotherapist to be a philosopher in an ancient mould but, like friends, we trust her or him to see a problem in the round. A "good relationship" between therapist and client appears to be one of the best predictors of a successful outcome and this is another obvious link between therapy and friendship. However, it is far from clear what makes a therapy relationship "good". This connection between two people is conceived differently by different schools of therapy.

One popular idea is that the therapist's role can be compared with that of a traditional healer or shaman who is able to divine the nature of a problem and supply a remedy. Another idea is that a therapist is like a parent figure who is able to correct the deficiencies of earlier mothering or fathering. Another opinion sets up the therapist as an expert with good relationships skills who can analyse and solve problems. All of these understandings of the therapist's role may contain an element of truth. A common thread running through them is that a therapist is technically proficient in some fashion or other. However, technical skill has little to do with our concept of an ideal friend. Friends are only secondarily valued for their skills; certain virtuous personal qualities seem to come first. As I show in the next chapter, written accounts of the ideals of friendship have been remarkably consistent over recorded history. Of course, a therapist who demonstrates the virtues of a friend could also be technically proficient in a manner that really helps us to solve a problem. Indeed, therapists are commonly sought out for their expertise. I suggest that a "good therapy relationship" combines both skills and virtues. Much of the therapy literature, which is vast, is heavily weighted on the skill element, as if its virtuous aspects are almost something to be ashamed of or disguised.

A book written some time ago by Paul Halmos, called *The Faith of the Counsellors*, pointed out the moral commitment, even faith, that, according to him, motivated counsellors in their work (a grouping for him that included all types of psychological therapist). Perhaps in order to emphasise that faith was needed, Halmos opened his book as follows:

> To advise people about their personal affairs has always been regarded as a thankless and futile task. (Halmos, 1965, p. 1)

With this remark, Halmos makes therapy continuous with everyday life and, by implication, with advice shared between friends. He doesn't try to explain his extreme pessimism about its outcome. Halmos argues that although counsellors do not care to admit it, they have to draw on faith when they deal with incorrigible clients and almost intractable problems. A "kind of stubborn confidence in the rightness of what they are doing" seems to be required. However, under the influence of science, suggests Halmos, "even charity and kindness must be planned, ordered, and scientifically controlled" (ibid., p. 13). In other words, what he would regard as *agape* has to be dressed up by counsellors themselves as a professional skill.

Perhaps Halmos intended to be provocative but the issues he raises are genuine ones. For instance, can loving and helping another ever be simulated and still retain their virtuous and inspiring qualities? If not, does this really matter if a client is happy with the result of therapy? Do techniques that require therapists to manipulate or disguise their own emotions have detrimental effects on their own well-being? For instance, Halmos refers to "synthetic parental loving" (ibid., p. 51) in which the expression of friendship is put forward as a technical device.

If Halmos is right that counsellors prefer to disguise their love and friendship, therapy must involve ambivalence and dissimilation. As he humorously puts it:

> The counsellor, though not at liberty to get a kick out of understanding and mastery, is still allowed to get a kick out of stopping himself getting a kick out of counselling. (Ibid., p. 79)

Halmos does not entirely condemn the performance of friendship. As he notes, we would not condemn the musician who manages to transport us to emotional heights through technical proficiency. He compares therapy with Stanislavski's method of acting:

> The counsellor's identification with the role he constantly plays results in a rare and impressive accumulation of a sympathetic and caring attitude towards others. (Ibid., p. 56)

At this point, I will leave open the question of whether therapists perform friendship or genuinely embody it. It is not as if we do not "perform" with our friends as well, and some sociologists have taken drama as their metaphor for understanding social life (Goffman, 1959). I will now briefly outline the assumptions of several popular conceptions of the therapist's role in order to contrast them with friendship.

Healer or shaman

An extremely influential source of the "healing" metaphor for therapy is Jerome Frank's idea that psychotherapy has much in common with traditional healing practices observed in societies all over the world

(Frank, 1973; Frank & Frank, 1993). This perspective is heavily endorsed by Bruce Wampold (2007, 2010), an eminent researcher in the field of psychotherapy. The conception of therapist as healer assumes that people seeking help acknowledge that they are troubled, even disordered, and in traditional societies, perhaps the victims of witchcraft or sorcery. The healer's formulation of the trouble, as viewed by modern proponents of the healing role, is to regard it as a culturally acceptable version of events. This is said to be accompanied by a ritual enactment of techniques that strengthens the credibility of the healer's explanation, thereby promoting an expectation in the client that benefit will eventually accrue. In other words, in this understanding of the therapist's role it is not what she or he specifically does to address a client's concern but, rather, it is a client's acceptance of an "adaptive explanation that is critical rather than the absolute truthfulness of the psychological explanation" (Wampold, 2007, p. 866).

I do not believe that many therapists would disagree with the proposition that they present themselves as credible and knowledgeable, that they engender hope of improvement, and that all of this helps to re-moralise a client. Nevertheless, the "therapy as healing ritual" account still strikes me as a rather cynical view, placing the therapist in the position of a charismatic salesperson. As Wampold writes, each and every therapeutic practice constitutes "convincing narratives that persuasively influence patients to accept more adaptive explanations for their disorders and take ameliorative actions" (ibid., p. 864). An assumption slipped into this argument is that a client is suffering from a "disorder" and is in a state of confusion about its cause. While I have met a few clients who fit this description, they are the exception. It is even occasionally the case that the problem, as a client presents it, fits the criteria for a psychiatric diagnosis and that it has been helpful to clarify or confirm this. However, I find myself more commonly expressing the view that to see oneself as mentally disordered is far from helpful. The analogy between rituals and a therapist's pronouncements and actions also lacks credibility. Clients have difficulties in the real world. Problems require considerable analysis, reflection, and difficult decisions. Solutions are hard-fought, not just passively accepted as a ritual to be undergone. If accepted at face value, the analogy with traditional healing amounts to a therapist acting in the role of magician. There is relatively little space for an emotional commitment to the client.

While adopting the healing metaphor for describing the therapist's role, Frank and Frank believe that clients perceive their therapist as someone who is "competent, genuinely cares about their welfare, and has no ulterior motives" (Frank & Frank, 1993, p. 40). This helpful stance towards a client can hardly be compared to some traditional healing practices where the entrails of an animal are examined or magical words are enunciated by a priest. The motives of a traditional healer may have little to do with caring, and the supplicant could well be feeling fear and awe.

It is true that certain techniques used in psychotherapy have a ritualistic quality, and they are also employed in a deliberately engineered "healing setting". The rationale for therapy may contain a fair amount of myth and hype. However, throughout their book, Frank and Frank vacillate between the idea that therapy is a form of healing (i.e., a "cure" or "symptom relief") and healing as a collaborative attempt to solve problems and overcome difficulties. To me, there is a world of difference between these two perspectives. Although clients might frame their depressed mood or phobia as a "symptom" for which a cure is sought, it is only a symptom in a metaphorical sense. There is no underlying disorder to be cured or healed, only a state of affairs with which a client is unhappy. More often than not, the alleged symptom is related to circumstances in a client's life that need addressing socially or psychologically. A client may of course opt for medication but in this case what is being offered (ostensibly) is a medicinal remedy not a form of psychological therapy.

Therapist as storyteller

Psychotherapy has been compared to a secular religion, each school pushing its own dogma and rites. For instance, David Pilgrim writes:

> Therapeutic orientations are merely different ways in which narratives about the self can be constructed. Currently, we have no benchmark to judge whether one narrative is better than another, and one may never appear. (Pilgrim, 1997, p. 135)

On the one hand, if by "narrative" is meant a story about what matters in life and how each person can meld their personal opportunities and resources into a good plot, there are grounds for accepting this formulation of what therapy is about. On the other hand, there are clearly a number of good stories to latch on to and it does matter which one you pick. Perhaps what is meant in this quotation is that despite a majority of therapists being concerned with the validity of their approach and their version of truth, these versions are merely "narratives" that cannot be compared for their truth value. Although this may be the case, each client's problem is unique and requires a specific solution. A therapist might impose the same narrative framework on each client but a general story is hardly the answer a client is looking for. As in the "shamanic" model, the narrative account seems to suggest that a therapist is placed in the position of a good storyteller, and perhaps a snake oil salesman to boot.

At a fundamental level, therapy is concerned with factual truth. Did something happen or did it not? Jeffrey Masson condemned Freud because he believed that Freud wilfully interpreted family incest and sexual abuse as a client's wishes or fantasies (Masson, 1992). As in friendship, we expect truthfulness in therapy. White lies are acceptable if they protect reputations and personal sensitivities but truth is expected when it really matters. We do not expect agreement on the nature of truth, or on the version of truth a friend or a therapist holds, but we do expect people to be truthful about their truths. We do not demand complete openness about what has happened to others in their past but if a friendship is predicated on a lie, or a client wilfully acts with deception and conceals crucial information from a therapist, it breaks one of the fundamental rules of both friendship and therapy. Friendship and therapy are also similar in the sense that a criminal offence is committed when financial benefit, sexual favours, or other advantages are obtained on the basis of falsely professed declarations.

The narrative view puts into question the need for scientific truth. It suggests that schools of therapy are engaged in pseudoscience when they attempt to find evidence for their foundational theories and techniques. Given the hundreds of scientific journals that are now devoted to areas of knowledge that are relevant to human problems, it seems churlish to dismiss them as providing only ideological support for a narrative conception of the good life. From this standpoint, it could be argued that Freud's understanding of unconscious determinants of slips of the tongue was part of his narrative, which was then swallowed whole by his clients. However, we know from cognitive science that Freud was correct in the sense that thought operates in ways that can only be inferred. There is indeed a realm of reality about which we cannot speak from experience (Claxton, 2005). It seems important to hold on to the idea that verifiable theoretical knowledge can be relevant to the solution of human problems. If a theory allows accurate predictions to be made about the causes of a problem, it deserves to be regarded as theory and not merely as another narrative.

Therapist as secular priest

A plausible ancestry for the social role of therapist has been sought in religious confession (Foucault, 1981). Richardson and Stewart (2009) make a convincing case that the confession of sins was one of the pathways that led to the modern secular practice of psychoanalysis. In monastic communities of the first half of the first millennium, confession was a public act. The sin caused a rift in the community, enacted by ostracism, which was only repaired when the penitent had publicly acknowledged wrongdoing. This public display began to be replaced by regular private spiritual counsel, which included the confession of relatively minor sins that did not affect the community as a whole. The written "penitentials" of the period adopted a medical analogy in which "the confessor became the physician and the sinner became the patient". Their guidance became "the health-giving medicine of souls" (Richardson & Stewart, 2009, p. 476). The investigation of sins and the search for a matching penance resembled a diagnostic interview of the mental states and the circumstances surrounding each symptom (sin). The facts had to be ferreted out through strategic questioning. Richardson and Stewart go on to argue that monastic practices diffused into popular culture and into confession as a routine requirement of the faithful.

The process of obtaining forgiveness was privatised in the thirteenth century when the priest acquired the power of unbinding the sinner through an act of absolution. This power was enacted on behalf of God and the Church. However, a private confessional booth did not become the norm until the sixteenth century, when they were designed so as not to allow any physical contact between priest and penitent. As today, there was a suspicion that sexual improprieties could take place otherwise. Foucault (1981) maintained that confession was about verbalising truth, which in practice often revolved around sexual desires and acts. By implication, anything that was non-verbalised became a sin.

To draw a parallel here with later psychoanalysis, the focus remained on sex and on non-verbalised (now considered to be unconscious) wishes and fantasies.

Of course, by the time we reach the modern period, an introspective self-examination does not necessarily carry with it self-denunciation. Quite the reverse is often expected: freedom from self-censorship. Nevertheless, the suggestion that there are strong commonalities between the techniques of confession and psychoanalysis is persuasive. It is no longer considered credible that a therapist is an authority on moral matters, but are we not all moralists in our dealings with others, especially our friends? Nearly all problems presented to a therapist have a moral dimension. Whether or not a therapist exerts moral authority depends largely on the style of therapy and perhaps a therapist's own personal preferences. A client may be in awe of the expert and a therapist may enjoy the opportunity to pass judgement. Although clients may divulge guilty secrets, the analogy between therapy and confession is rather loose. Secrets are also shared between friends without necessarily the expectation or desire for a relief of guilt about wrongdoing. In a therapy context, confessing a "guilty secret" may or may not be related to moral or religious sentiments.

Therapist as technician

As I have already remarked, viewing therapy as a friendship-like relationship does not mean that there is no place for technical skill. Even the strongest advocates of this approach accept that an application of technique cannot be divorced from the context of a bond between two human beings. However, for the technically inclined, there is a tendency to see the normative enactment of friendship as convertible into a set of skills. There are several professional and social forces pushing the definition of therapy in this direction. The most compelling is the idea that therapy is concerned with mental health, in other words, curing people of their disorders or mental illnesses, which would appear to be a technical task. In my view, this medical perspective fits best with the idea of a therapist as healer or shaman (see above). The concept of mental disorder attributes human suffering to underlying dysfunctions of the mind or body, whether these be unconscious complexes, faulty habits, or a brain process. These attributions naturally lend themselves to formulating the goals of therapy in terms amenable to technical influence.

A second driver pushing therapy in a technical direction has a more convincing rationale. There are simply hundreds of different kinds of human problem and personal suffering. The craft skills and theoretical knowledge needed to deal with one kind of problem may have little in common with those needed for another. Consider, for example, advising a parent about caring for an autistic child, helping a gambler to overcome a compulsion to bet, assisting a person who is unable to find a partner, or reducing someone's urge to check repeatedly that gas taps are switched off. These are extremely diverse problems. While a friendship-like bond with a client may be necessary, it is unlikely to be sufficient, any more than blood-letting with leeches was sufficient for a variety of ills in the early history of medicine. It makes sense for clients to seek out therapists who are familiar with the kind of problem for which they seek help and who possess a certain degree of expertise in finding solutions to it.

A common sense approach to suffering would be to focus on what appears to be causing it, and I can see little justification for grouping the problems that beset human beings under one umbrella. A general science of psychopathology or mental ill-health does not seem to have a rational basis. The presumption of an underlying "disorder" is a lazy way of understanding the causes of suffering. A disorder label just gives the impression of an explanation. Trichotillomania (compulsive hair pulling) is a case in point. However, without resorting to a disorder model, it seems entirely reasonable to suppose that the social, biological, and physical sciences, philosophy, and cultural knowledge in general, have great potential for understanding and remedying the causes of human suffering.

Therapist as friend

My suggestion that a therapist is "a special kind of friend" is hardly new. It is implied in the writings of many therapists. They would agree that what they do is continuous with everyday life. They see themselves as in the business of transforming the ordinary into something creative and interesting:

> The happiness of dialogues is their power to refreshen, to bring about joy, to dissolve burdens and oppressions. (Riikonen & Vataja, 1999, p. 185)

This "happy dialogue" does have definite rules and boundaries, but it strongly resembles the way that authors from classical times up until the present day have written about the benefits of friendship. A few contemporary psychotherapists are clear about the similarities. Robert Hobson gives as one of the reasons for writing his book *Forms of Feeling: The Heart of Psychotherapy*, "I write for anyone who hopes to respond to a close friend, a student, or a little-known neighbour asking for help with a problem" (1994, p. xii). Mark Aveline (2005) uses the following words to describe the attributes of a model therapist: truth-telling, compassionate, kind, trustworthy, adaptable in wanting the best for the other, free of envy, encouraging, humble, and optimistic about the human condition. These sound like the qualities we look for in a friend.

The service of a professional is rarely the first port of call for help because most people sort out a problem on their own. In an early review of the available research evidence on the outcome of psychotherapy, spanning the 1950s and 1960s, Allen Bergin came to the conclusion that thirty per cent of people assigned to a treatment comparison group (that is, people who had not received professional help) no longer considered themselves to be in need of it when followed up later. Bergin was convinced that "psychotherapy is merely a special case of a much broader range of therapeutic phenomena that exist naturalistically in society" (Bergin, 1971, p. 246).

The need for professional therapy arises because the natural forms of therapeutic help are not uniformly helpful. Friends may be unavailable because they are wrapped up in their own concerns. To admit to having a problem can also put a person in a one-down position. He might prefer "to keep up appearances" rather than admit to needing advice. Therapy aspires to create a relationship that avoids some of these pitfalls. A psychotherapist does not gloat over your misfortune in the way that a friend might (secretly) do. Some therapists present themselves as trainers, educators, or coaches to play down the intimacy of their help, because clients may be more comfortable with the idea of it as a business transaction.

Jeffrey Masson is a severe critic of psychotherapy but he also cites research to suggest that a good therapist "is a keenly attentive, interested, benign and concerned listener—a friend who is warm and natural, is not averse to giving direct advice, who speaks one's language, makes sense, and rarely arouses intense anger" (1988, p. 289). As someone who trained as a psychoanalyst and later rejected his profession, Masson reflects that, "any advice I had to offer would be no better than that of a well-informed friend" (ibid., p. 299). Masson therefore endorses the notion that friendship has the potential to be beneficial, although delivered up in the form of therapy, he seems to believe, like Halmos, that advice is doomed to be thankless or futile, and, according to him, frequently harmful.

In my view, there are distinct advantages in an honest contractual relationship with a person who stands outside all other relationships in one's life. Friends take sides, as any divorced couple know. Although there are risks in consulting an "expert", these are compensated by hearing the opinion of a neutral outsider. A client can treat a therapist as a friend without expecting, or offering, to fulfil all of the usual obligations of friendship. It is undeniable that a therapist is compensated for her services. Contact with a client is strictly regulated to occur at designated times. These are important differences but they do not necessarily undermine other commitments. An examination of ethical guidelines produced by professional associations reveals the importance they attach to maintaining distance from a close, friendly relationship, while not at the same time denying it. Codes of conduct go to great lengths and in minute detail to say why therapy is not friendship. All these protestations simply reinforce the fact that in some important sense it is.

In the end, a therapist, like a friend, will not let you down. In the *Standards of Conduct, Performance and Ethics* produced by a British regulator of the practice of health professionals, it is stated:

> You must act in the best interests of service users ... You must protect service users if you believe that any situation puts them in danger. This includes the conduct, performance or health of a colleague. The safety of service users must come before any personal or professional loyalties at all times. (HCPC, 2015, p. 8)

These guidelines do not make clear what danger, safety, and personal and professional loyalties really amount to in practice, but the implication seems to be that the professional will put herself on the line if she feels strongly that a client is getting a raw deal. In reality, this is a heavy responsibility; whistle-blowers are frequently at risk of losing their job.

Therapists are likely to describe what they offer as "empathy", "care", or "support" rather than anything as strong as "love". Even close friends hesitate to speak of love although the etymological root of the word "friend" is Anglo-Saxon "freond", and "freon" meant "to love". People may be reluctant to mention their esteem for a friendship because there is no written guarantee of its solidity or permanence. I therefore view friendship as an ideal, comprising a set of virtues that we would all like to live up to but sometimes fail to fulfil. If therapy were to be viewed merely as a technology, without the commitment normally associated with friendship, it would cease to exist in a recognisable form. It would dissolve into a depersonalised relationship, no longer a special bond between particular persons but a service rather like that provided by dentists, beauticians, or personal trainers. This is not to say that people occupying these roles never become friends but to suggest that they can do a good job without becoming friends. They may be friendly but I do not take friendliness to signify friendship; rather, this word seems to mean "acting like" (or simulating) a friend.

It is only in the last couple of decades that social psychologists have begun to take a serious interest in the kind of love that friendship fosters or embodies (Fehr, Sprecher & Underwood, 2008). They refer to it as "compassionate love". They define it as a form of love that is chosen, not out of a sense of duty or for what it supplies in return, but as a discerning form of empathy. Its ultimate intention is the good of the other, which may mean weighing up matters in order to make the right decision. Consequently, it may include "tough love" and a balancing of one's needs with that of the other. At its heart, there is the humanist value of respecting the other person as a whole.

The official designation for people who use the British NHS mental health services is "service user" rather than "patient", as has traditionally been the case. This seems to indicate a trend towards a more impersonal and technical conception of the services provided. I think it unlikely that a client of a therapist would regard the term "service user" as a suitable portrayal of their relationship, and a therapist may be unhappy to see their role simply as a "service provider". The new terminology clearly downplays the personal bond that exists between therapist and client. A bond of friendship between the advice giver and taker may not be needed for some therapy services; for instance, a programme of advice for smoking cessation could be administered effectively without it. I do not insist on a strict boundary around the edges of the concept of friend and therapist. Nevertheless, at their centre, both share similar values.

Implications of therapy as friendship

If therapy is similar to friendship, both types of relationship share all the intuitive perceptions and judgements we routinely make about other people. In fact, empathy with a client would be impossible without them. Theorists of psychotherapy would argue that they have gone a long way in making the interpersonal more understandable. However, these theorists probably underestimate the extent to which therapists can rise above intuitive assumptions and adopt an impartial and neutral stance. They may also underestimate the extent to which a client is be able to sense a therapist's moral position on a problem as the client presents it. Values are revealed by tone of voice, facial expression, and other subtle cues. However, unlike a friend, who may express an opinion regardless of how it is expected to be received, a therapist aims to be impartial. This professional behaviour makes it unlike friendship, as therapists are far more concerned about the consequences of what they say or do, especially with a care not to cause harm.

Apart from having good intentions, a therapist usually aims for moral neutrality in the sense of not overtly approving or disapproving a particular course of action (unless consistent with sought-after advice or a client's own decisions). However, it is unlikely that a therapist would be led by a client into colluding with values that he could not endorse himself. Therapists have different philosophies and values. Some show absolute respect for a client's self-determination while others take a utilitarian attitude, assuming that this is shared by a client. They may instruct a client to follow a course of action (or undergo a technique) designed to be "beneficial", an outcome which a client may take on trust. Understandably, critics of therapy have been sensitive about respecting a client's opinion. When first introduced, behavioural techniques, based upon theories of learning, were described by some as "brainwashing". Other therapies were called "non-directive" because they avoided giving direct advice.

While naturally holding on to their own set of values, therapists cannot function without respecting a client's moral position. This does not necessarily mean accepting it, and differences, as with friendship, can be expected. When a client asks for guidance, it seems best to offer a point of view rather than pretend that neutrality is possible. We live in a society in which different values are normally tolerated. Adults take responsibility for their actions and they are rewarded or punished for what they themselves initiate. The initial stage of therapy is often a kind of negotiation about the desirability of various goals. Just as friends do not usually launch in with a heavy-handed riposte to the presentation of a problem, this negotiation needs to be handled with delicacy. Occasionally, there is a moral issue that cannot be sidestepped and professional codes of ethics provide guidelines for dealing with these dilemmas, citing circumstances in which a therapist's (and society's) values can be imposed against a client's wishes.

Thus, therapy has to weave a precarious path between respect for a client's autonomy and an explicit intention to exercise an influence. The imbalance of power for which therapy has been criticised is normal and need not be regarded as a form of abuse. Clients are usually looking for a new perspective, and given that there is rarely only one solution to a problem, therapists may be able to open up new possibilities from which clients can take their pick. In this manner, a client remains responsible and autonomous. The result can be a "dance", sometimes sparring, but this is inevitable in a practice where there are no obviously right or wrong solutions to a problem.

Clients choose their friends and, if they are wise, they will also choose their therapist. There are moves by government bodies to give the stamp of approval to certain therapeutic techniques in the way that new pharmaceutical products are approved as "safe" and efficacious. However, in the final analysis, entering therapy means taking a personal risk because we have not yet reached a stage (if we ever do) where therapy can guarantee a desired outcome.

Attitudes towards seeking help vary considerably. The tough-minded believe that people are the architects of their own problems and they may avoid therapy altogether. The tender-minded are more likely to perceive external causes of misfortune and welcome assistance. Criticism of what therapy sets out to achieve has sometimes come from professionals themselves but chiefly from sociologists and other commentators. For the tough-minded, therapy is a form of self-indulgence that encourages a flabby, weak-willed attitude to life. For tender-minded critics, therapy turns a blind eye to the "real social causes" of problems and gives too much credence to "experts". The growth in the number of personal advisors has become a topic for serious debate in sociology. Discussion of these various issues is essentially about social and moral values, rather than about therapy's effectiveness.

If therapy is a form of friendship, both parties need to be protected from its intimacies. Professional codes of conduct are designed with this in mind. Clients can be exploited, but therapists too are vulnerable to the temptation of subjugating their own needs in order to satisfy their urge to be helpful. They have to maintain an upbeat narrative while listening to tales of woe. On occasion, doing therapy can feel like carrying another's burden while being impotent to make a difference. In a later chapter, I discuss therapist "burnout" and how professional conduct should be regulated, bearing in mind that therapy is not a service like podiatry or the prescription of a hearing aid. At present, the best advice to potential clients is "buyer beware", given that therapy cannot guarantee a satisfactory outcome, let alone a "cure". Both client and therapist bear responsibility for making change happen but opinion differs as to who is accountable for success or failure.

Different approaches to therapy

I have classified therapy into three main approaches (Chapters Three, Four and Five). Each of them has discernible roots in the history and philosophy of Western culture but it is only in the last century that they have crystallised as "schools" that enter into disputes and argue over their differences. The strategy I use to present the approaches is to combine broad generalisations about philosophies and values with quotations from significant authors, historical and contemporary, who explain what it means to change or be changed. Their quoted words bring to life the philosophical abstractions and highlight the psychological position of the agent of change, the therapist. I focus mainly on early exponents of an approach because this exaggerates the fault lines between different schools. The assumptions and values of the pioneers are still quite evident in modern transformations of earlier practices but the current scene is characterised by diversity and a mingling of methods. It could be argued that there are no longer any distinct schools of therapy but this is not the case, and the argument is perhaps motivated by a wish for empirical research to decide what "works" and what "doesn't". In this book, I argue that this faith in "evidence" is deeply entangled with its own value judgements.

I will discuss the humanistic approach first because, in my view, it is an expression of a longer-term historical trend than either the psychodynamic or technical/applied science approaches. Since the Renaissance and the rise of Humanism, people have placed increasing value on autonomy and self-reflection. What they decide to do depends more on impulses coming from within than on guidance from without coming from "authorities", spiritual or secular. More and more of us seem to be thinking about the choices we make and what we want to get out of life. In large measure, this explains the rise in popularity of professional helpers and also self-help in its various guises.

I will consider psychodynamic approaches next, partly in deference to their historical significance. However, Freud's original theories have been substantially modified, if not almost entirely replaced, and the practice of psychoanalysis in the traditional sense of lying on a couch three times a week for a number of years is now available only to the very few. My third approach, technology and applied science has, by contrast, gone from strength to strength. It has responded to pressures from policymakers and health providers to produce evidence and demonstrate value for money. It can also claim considerable success in developing techniques to overcome certain common types of problem. However, it is not my intention to show that one approach is more effective than another. Rather, I critically examine the values and aims of each approach, and also the whole endeavor to prove "effectiveness".

CHAPTER TWO

A brief historical survey of wise counsel and friendship

My aim in this chapter is to show that there is continuity between the way friendship has been described in historical sources and how the therapy relationship is understood in contemporary society.

Writings from the classical period suggest that friendship was held in high esteem but there is less evidence for the way ordinary people—who were neither kinsfolk nor tied by other obligations—actually turned to each other for support or advice. With increasing literacy, people could express their friendship by writing letters, and now, of course, with the telephone and digital communication, contact is so much easier, transforming what it means to have a circle of friends.

My survey will begin with an examination of some guidance written for parish priests in the early fifteenth century because, almost incidentally, it reveals how a priest's pastoral role was similar to that of a contemporary therapist. The priest must have had friendly relationships with his parishioners, sharing their everyday problems and also dealing with their suffering and emotional needs. Clearly, as now, people sometimes dealt with moral dilemmas by giving in to temptation. Although the ensuing fear and guilt could be remedied (at least in part) by the act of confession and absolution, John Myrc's guide for parish priests (written in the 1400s and reproduced 1902) reveals his sensitivity to the task of influencing others for their own salvation. In many ways, the guide is equivalent to a modern therapy manual. It was designed for those parish priests "who had no book of their own" and for others of "mene lore" (i.e., of only common knowledge of precepts).

For the confessant, a priest was not a spiritual equal and, in this sense, not a friend. Moreover, confession was a religious duty, not a "helpful" way of unburdening guilt. However, a priest encouraged honest communication and could provide support. Myrc's guide, written in Middle English in the form of a poem, is extremely practical, a good, "hands on" piece of advice. It is structured around receiving a confession in private, handing out a penance, and giving absolution of sins in the form of a ritual recital of words spoken in Latin. At the same time, and more or less incidentally, Myrc reveals a code of ethics that regulated his role.

Like a modern professional who would not want a client to be obtaining therapy elsewhere at the same time, the priest's role was expected to be exclusive. The priest was advised not to hear the confession of a person from another parish unless he knew that the parishioner's own priest was unethical because he did not ensure confidentiality, that is, he could not be relied upon to be discreet. There were other exceptions: if the sin concerned the other priest's kinsfolk or if that priest "by any of hys paresch have layn" (ibid., p.23). Like modern therapists, some priests became sexually intimate with their "clients" and could no longer be trusted.

Myrc advises caution when a priest hears a confession from a woman. The priest is not to look her in the face and should sit "still as a stone", and "neither cough nor spit" (ibid., p. 24). If she hesitates, he should encourage her to speak boldly, saying he has perhaps sinned as badly or worse. In modern terms, he encourages genuine and empathic communication. If the sin is lechery, he asks if it was with her consent or if she was raped, whether she did it out of fear or for money. There was no requirement to name the other person "unless it be needful" (ibid., p. 45), and a woman's penance must be such that "her husband may not know" (ibid., p. 47). There seems to be practical wisdom behind all this. If the woman carries out her penance, there is no need to stir up further trouble. Like a modern therapist, the priest is attempting to manage a complex moral situation with finesse.

For a reluctant confessant, the priest will say, "Tell me what is in your thoughts", and then, if she is not forthcoming, issue the following reproof: "And when thou herest how hast do, knowlache well a-non thereto" (That is, when you hear yourself telling what you have done, you will instantly acknowledge it (ibid., p. 25). The priest handles a delicate situation, not with threats, but with gentle persuasion. The priest then runs through a checklist of common sins, from manslaughter through to going to the ale house on holy days, leaving a farm gate open, or riding through corn. Compared to the present day, there was considerable emphasis on the sin of pride (claiming to be better than you were in terms of your abilities), or boasting about your special links with the higher echelons of society ("that thou art trusted by lady or lord", ibid., p. 31). To neglect one's religious duties was a sin but so also was to be "slow to help thy wife to what she had need of" (ibid., p. 34). In fact, quite a few family situations are alluded to, such as quarrelling with one's wife and "keeping thy children in subjection" (ibid., p. 42). For a mother to "over lyth'" her child (in other words, smother it by having it in bed with her, ibid., p. 42) was classified along with murder and referred upwards to the bishop, as were those who had lain with their sisters or cousins (committed incest).

Penances were finely judged to be practically efficacious. Since some parishioners do not tell all their sins, care must be taken to find them out. A person has to be "in their wits" (know what she is doing), and wisdom is needed in dealing with "manhede" (madness) lest the person is sent into wickedness or to the devil. A lighter penance is given if a person is sorry, and a heavier one if "stiff of heart". However, the severity of a penance was carefully calculated, "for if a man has more laid on him than he will do, he will cast it all aside and be worse than if he had not gone to confession" (ibid., p. 47). It seems that the priest had to exercise considerable understanding of a kind that we would now call psychological. Each sin had its own remedy, *viz.* pride its opposite, meekness: "to kiss the earth and look on dead man's bones" (ibid., p. 48). A person in a state of wrath should, "see how angels flee from him and fiends run fast to him and burn his heart with hellfire" (ibid., p. 48).

We can see from Myrc's book that the priest had to exercise "person management skills" as well as carry out formal religious rites. He did not tread on the toes of fellow priests and knew when to refer upwards in the case of more serious forms of deviance. He acted in strict confidence (unless it was "needful" to act otherwise) and he did not stir up trouble if at all possible. He dealt with the daily problems of quarrelling families, child abuse, and marital infidelities. The techniques at his disposal were limited (confession, penance, absolution) but he attempted to exercise them with practical wisdom. It is clear that there is a discernible priestly ancestry in the role of therapist that is not of a strictly spiritual nature.

Turning now to friendship and its relationship to counselling and support, there are many texts from antiquity that describe its nature. I will take the Renaissance as a convenient starting point. In any case, thinkers at this time drew heavily upon classical sources. Francis Bacon and Michel de Montaigne wrote essays on friendship in the late 1500s that were enormously influential at the time and remain so. What they had to say about friendship is relevant to a discussion of close helping relationships of the kind found in contemporary therapy.

Bacon first published his essays in 1597 and an enlarged edition appeared in 1625 (Bacon, 1920). He reminds us that solitude can be had in a crowd and that talk is but a "Tinckling Cymball where there is no Love"(ibid., p. 76). He depicts friendship as a special loving relationship, whose main fruit is the "Ease and Discharge of the Fulness and Swellings of the Heart, which Passions of all kinds doe cause and induce" (ibid., p. 77). Bacon resorts to an analogy with physical remedies to describe the benefits but he is unequivocal that opening your heart, and whatever oppresses it, to a friend is a type of "Civill Shrift or Confession", not treatment from a physician (ibid., p. 77). Here he makes a direct link to the priestly role. As we would say in the language of today, Bacon singles out the psychological effects of relating to a sympathetic person and points out the benefits of dialogue. He finds it strange that even the very powerful rate friendship so highly that they will put themselves at risk and inconvenience. They are required to "raise" subjects or servants into "companions" and "almost Equals" (ibid., p. 77). He says that the Roman name for these people were *Participes Curarum* or partners in care. Bacon sums up the first fruit of friendship as the redoubling of joys and the cutting of griefs in half.

Bacon emphasises equality as one of the foundations of friendship. Without it, the relationship would risk being exploitative. The powerful have to "raise up" others to their level. In a relationship of unequal power, there would, presumably, exist motives to flatter or manipulate for personal advantage.

Therapists do not need reminding of their potential power and they attempt to guard against its misuse. Beyond their personal benefit through financial gain, therapists have created strict rules to prohibit other forms of exchange or personal advantage. Their aim seems to be to strive towards an equal relationship in which there is at least a possibility for honest feedback and unfeigned love.

The second fruit of friendship, says Bacon, is its supremely beneficial effect on the "Understanding", removing the "Darknesse and Confusion of Thoughts". Although a person can attempt to think things through alone, "Communicating and discoursing with another" makes it easier to toss thoughts around, marshal them, and "seeth how they look when they are turned into Words". According to Bacon, friends are the best vehicle for this process but a person can do it alone, and "bringeth his owne Thoughts to Light, and whetteth his Wits against a Stone, which it selfe cuts not" (ibid., p. 81). He suggests that it is better to tell your thoughts to a statue than to suppress them. However, Bacon notes that a person's own thoughts are likely to be "infused and drenched in his Affections and Customs" (ibid., p.81), in other words, they are a product of habit and emotional investments. Faithful counsel from a friend is "Drier and purer", because it is more likely to be objective or impartial. A person's own self is a "Flatterer", whereas the freedom of speech and frankness of a friend offers a remedy against this. A friend can draw attention to the morality of acts, in contrast to reading books about morality which Bacon feels is "a little Flat and Dead" (ibid., p. 81).

The last fruit of friendship is "Aid" and "Bearing a Part in all Actions and Occasions" (ibid., p. 83). A friend is a kind of extension of yourself who looks after your interests, such as making sure that after your death, a child is bestowed in marriage. A friend can praise your merits whereas it might be unseemly to do so yourself. A person is limited in what he can say and do by reason of his role, as father, husband, etc., but a friend can be deputised to convey a message. In modern terms, we would say that a friend can act as an advocate. Therapists frequently fulfil this role too.

Bacon highlights an aspect of seeking counsel that all therapists would endorse. This is to seek a friend who is "wholly acquainted with a Man's Estate". To seek advice here and there risks being distracted and misled rather than being counselled "Settle and Direct". He reminds the reader that seeking advice from various quarters is like having a disease and calling in a physician who is otherwise "unacquainted with your body" (ibid., p. 82). He follows this up with the probable outcome: "And so cure the Disease, and kill the Patient." In a similar way, a therapist makes sure to perform a rounded assessment so that whatever other help being provided is compatible with her own attempt to change the presenting problem.

Montaigne's essay "Of friendship", originally published in 1580, is largely a tribute to a particular friend, Étienne de la Boétie, but we thereby discover how he compares friendship with other kinds of relationship (Montaigne, 1877). For instance, Montaigne mentions marriage in order to highlight its different character. Marriage is a covenant "which is free but the continuance in it forced and compulsory", a state of affairs that may "divert the current of a lively affection". By contrast, friendship is concerned only with itself, something which he feels is "full and perfect" and unlikely to be found with a woman, least of all in a marriage (ibid., Book 1, chapter 27).

He also points out that a child and his parent cannot be friends by reason of the inequality that exists between them; the child should be respectful and the parent must sometimes admonish. Presumably, as the child matures, and is treated more as an equal, the relationship can develop into friendship. However, according to Montaigne, any family tie has the potential to weaken friendship where there is a conflict of interest.

The question of equality in a therapy relationship is a subject about which there is currently some disagreement. Certain critics would argue that therapy is intrinsically a relationship of unequal power, and on these grounds it cannot be compared with friendship. Like a parent, a therapist is understood to have a socially sanctioned role. In response, it could be said that inequalities exist in any relationship, and people respect one another for their talents, which are often unequal, without necessarily creating a feeling that this puts a person at any disadvantage. Inequality in status or power would only nullify a friendship if an unfair advantage were taken.

Montaigne regards friendship as a relationship of constancy, trust, and mutual obligation, in which there is no pay-off in terms of pleasure, profit, public or private interest. Unlike marriage, there is nothing forced or compulsory about it. He admits that marriage doesn't suit him because he hates "all sorts of obligation and restraint" (ibid., chapter 5). However, he writes that when a friend's welfare is considered as highly as one's own, or a friend is considered to be an extension of oneself, friendship does not entail any "obligation" to give because the benefit to the friend is experienced equally in oneself.

In some other essays, Montaigne's remarks about friendship are less high-flown. When discoursing on the art of discussion his chief emphasis is on truth:

> We evade correction, whereas we ought to offer and present ourselves to it, especially when it appears in the form of conference, and not of authority ... I could suffer myself to be rudely handled by my friend, so much as to tell me that I am a fool, and talk I know not of what ... we must fortify and harden our hearing against this tenderness of the ceremonious sound of words ... When any one contradicts me, he raises my attention, not my anger ... I hail and caress truth in what quarter soever I find it. (Book 3, chapter 8)

In these words, we hear Montaigne's greater emphasis on truth from his friends instead of their support and love, as with Bacon. In the words of Oscar Wilde, a few centuries later, a friend "is one who stabs you in the front" (Quoted in Grayling, 2013, p. 10). Montaigne claims to gain more from a feeling of mastery over himself when he is challenged than he does from a victory over others. He wants plain speaking, not bookishness. Nevertheless, he argues that any challenge should be civilized and orderly. Montaigne's sentiments chime with the values of humanistic therapy in which a therapist is advised to be "genuine" rather than merely technically skilled, and should aim for truth, while respecting a client's own way of searching for it. It seems safe to assume that most clients would prefer their therapist to express truthful opinions. They might not accept what they hear but they will probably want to think about it. The dialogue is instructive, even combative, as it was for Montaigne.

In the century that followed Francis Bacon's main works, the Duc de la Rochefoucauld's maxims, published between 1665 and 1678 (La Rochefoucauld, 1959) further developed Bacon's insights on self-flattery. His writings took the form of a collection of aphorisms that have the knack of revealing the self-interest that underlies friendship and romantic love. For instance, he seems to be speaking directly to therapists when he writes:

> We all have strength enough to endure the troubles of others. (Ibid., No. 19)

I read his intention as not simply to play the cynic but to reinforce what we value as the true fruits of friendship. For him, brutal honesty was necessary to discover who we really are, to become aware that we are more than game-players who dissimulate to gain advantage. Bacon had pointed out that friends can see through our self-serving prejudices but La Rochefoucauld ratchets up the awareness:

> If we never flattered ourselves, we should get very little pleasure indeed. (Ibid., No. 123)

He also goes further in seeming to imply that we can only be an authentic self when we cease to be selfishly motivated. When we lie to others, we lose contact with who we really are:

> We are so used to disguising ourselves from others that we end by disguising ourselves from ourselves. (Ibid., No. 119)

Therapy seems to offer the opportunity of being brutally honest with ourselves. The rules for civilised self-presentation can be relaxed. Friends may be able to supply these opportunities as well, but more often than not we are concerned that they will take advantage or lose their good opinion of us. It is not without reason that therapy offers one of the fruits of friendship without these risks. La Rochefoucauld says that we must trust friends come what may, but in the seventeenth century he had little alternative:

> It is more shameful to distrust one's friends than to be deceived by them. (Ibid., No. 110)

In his succinct review of friendship, Anthony Grayling claims that reciprocity is an indispensable part of its nature (2013, p. 172). One implication of this view is that the therapy relationship, in which there is a clearly defined giver and taker, is not friendship and should therefore be described as one between patron and client. In reality, therapy is not a straightforward commercial transaction. In fact, it is common for a client to restore the norm of reciprocity by offering a therapist a gift (see Chapter Eleven). I suggest that a therapist does give something of a personal nature. Consequently, whether or not to accept a gift is one of the boundaries of therapy that has given rise to much debate.

Grayling considers whether friendship is motivated by a benevolent concern for all fellow human beings but he feels that this kind of love would be stretching accepted notions of friendship too far. The same would probably be said of the motivations of most therapists, but perhaps a benevolent concern for all, driven by a religious belief that everyone is deserving of love, does play a part in the motivation of some. This view is compatible with the idea that when religion was challenged by science in the nineteenth century, people anchored themselves in the certainties of science while transforming universal benevolence into a drive for welfare and social reform. Therapy is, after all, provided by the welfare state in order to increase the general fund of happiness. In fact, a new breed of "well-being practitioners" has recently been created by the UK Government.

Grayling makes the point that romantic love is something else again, and few therapists would disagree with that. Nevertheless, neither friends, therapists, nor clients are immune to romance (see Chapter Seven).

Grayling does not underplay the role of a mutual trade-off in friendship. There is usually some advantage to be had in addition to mutual pleasure and enjoyment. Friends share burdens and difficulties despite the fact that the distribution of benefits may be uneven. When friendship is valued for its own sake, as a good in its own right, a strict trade-off interpretation does not do it justice. In any case, friends are often made on the basis of instant attraction. Friendship may bestow advantages but when these appear to be calculated, especially in a concealed way, they may ruin a friendship.

Therapy departs from the norms of friendship because there is payment for a service. However, the financial benefit to a therapist (if he abides by professional ethics) does not involve deception, dishonesty, or concealment. The benefit to the therapist is transparent, and so the client can (to a large degree) discount it when viewing him as a kind of friend. In my view, although therapy has a commercial basis, it would not be successful or ethical if the motivation to provide it were solely financial. For instance, if therapists were to be paid by results, it would significantly alter the nature of the relationship. Therapists take on clients when, actuarially, it could be demonstrated that the probability of success is rather low. As Halmos (1965) points out, they are willing to work with difficult problems and unmotivated clients, and this tokens a kind of faith or commitment.

Even when the probability of a successful outcome is high, a therapist is likely to be more successful when he finds something to like about his client (see Chapter Seven). Without empathy, it would be difficult to work. This personal connection can take the form of a battle or a common campaign, but both connections are "real". I suggest that a client is more likely to change when she feels that a therapist is rooting for her rather than going through the motions of carrying out an "effective technique".

CHAPTER THREE

The humanistic approach

The growth of humanism over the last millennium is best summed up by an increasing understanding of a human being as a whole person or self, defined by her inner experiences, her beliefs, and by her capacity to choose rationally rather than in accordance with a higher power or the dictates of some *part* of herself, such as her genes, her instinctual motivations, or her habits. Although it is an anti-mechanistic approach, it does not deny that biology is an essential part of our make-up. It is best viewed as beginning at a higher level at which people experience each other and respond to each other as whole persons. By contrast, psychodynamic and scientific/technical approaches are essentially concerned with a causal understanding of human beings. For them, expert knowledge and specialised techniques are seen as important in helping a person to change. For the humanistic therapist, only the client himself can be the expert on what he "knows" through experience, and what sense he wants to make of it. The therapist respects the unique truths of the other person while attempting to be true to her own experience.

Historical figures who exemplify the tradition

Beatrice Webb

Beatrice Webb was never a therapist but she was a contemporary of Freud and wrote with great insight about what it is like for a humanist to attempt to understand another person. Webb was a social reformer, socialist, and one of the founders of the London School of Economics (Webb, 1938). While Freud was working out his theories, a nineteen-year-old Beatrice was planning to be an "applied sociologist". She wanted to understand people in their social setting, using methods of observation, interviews, and note-taking. Her thoughts on this subject (which led later to her work with London's poor) cast an interesting light on values that are now taken for granted within social science research and therapy. Nothing could be further from the psychoanalytic couch than Webb's manner of gaining information about the inner and outer promptings of another person's words and actions. Her style was undoubtedly humanistic, respectful and, as far as possible, impartial in the sense of not wanting to allow her own biases to get in the way of her objectivity.

She placed value on "the person" and a person's right to choose but, at the same time, assumed that critical thinking and empirical evidence was the right basis for choice. Webb avoided high-flown theory, and her relationship with those she met was built on common sense, respect for another's point of view, and a genuinely felt concern. In words taken from her diaries she writes:

> I would like to go amongst men and women with a determination to know them; to humbly observe and consider their characteristics; always remembering how much there is in the most inferior individual which is outside and beyond one's understanding. Every fresh intimacy strengthens the conviction of one's own powerlessness to comprehend fully any other nature, even when one watches it with love. And without sympathy there is an impassable barrier to the real knowledge of the inner workings which guide the outer actions of human beings. Sympathy, or rather accepted sympathy is the only instrument for the dissection of character. All great knowers and describers of human nature must have possessed this instrument. The perfection of the instrument depends no doubt on a purely intellectual quality, analytical imagination—this again,

> originating in subjective complexity of motive and thought. But unless this latter quality is possessed to an extraordinary degree, insight into other natures is impossible, unless we subordinate our interest in self and its workings to a greater desire to understand others. (Diary entry, 1883, ibid., p. 141)

In this passage, Webb emphasises the central role of reciprocity and an accepting relationship. It acknowledges, too, "analytical imagination" and subordination of "the needs of the self" in the service of this understanding. In her everyday life at the time, as described in her diary, Webb was obliged to go through the motions of fulfilling her social obligations, chiefly with other society women and her father's business and political friends. In commenting on this, she highlights another quality admired by later humanistic therapists—authenticity:

> But it is a curious experience moving about among men and women, talking much, as you are obliged to do, and never mentioning those thoughts and problems which are your real life, and which absorb, in their pursuit and solution, all the earnestness of your nature. This doubleness of motive, still more this dissemblance towards the world you live in, extending even to your own family must bring with it a feeling of unreality; worse a loss of energy in the sudden transitions from the one life to the other. (Diary entry, 1883, ibid., p. 144).

Webb is here noting the potential perils of observing others, however worthy the motive, for one's own authentic sense of self. To accept the reality of others can lead you to question your own reality, with a potentially enervating effect. You help others to express their authentic being while attempting to preserve your own. To engage in this kind of relationship is to be willing to accept a degree of self-denial, or "dissemblance" as Webb puts it. A therapist may need to bridge a wide psychological gap across mentality or culture; the distance must increase considerably when a therapist is working in, say, a prison and relating to a murderer or paedophile.

When Webb looks back in 1926 to the faith of late Victorian scientists, she shrewdly observes that a new motive was added to a belief in science: "the transference of the emotion of self-sacrificing service from God to man" (Ibid., p.153). Most therapists probably do not act out of religious faith. Freud saw himself as guided by science, a position shared with modern technical therapists. It is important to ask what motivates therapists to occupy their chosen slot in society. It cannot be dismissed that they are driven by a desire to put the world to rights, not by direct political action, but through the values that guide their personal relationships. In order to do so, according to Webb, they may have to subjugate their own needs.

Although Webb wanted to be an applied scientist, she did not follow the path that would eventually lead, in the latter half of the twentieth century, to the application of techniques based on scientific principles and empirical research. Her values were centred on people and her relationship with them, rather than on utilitarian justifications for action. In any case, she was doubtful about the scope of scientific understanding in relation to human affairs. She wrote:

> There was one riddle in the application of the scientific method which continuously worried me, and which still leaves me doubtful. Can the objective method, pure and undefiled, be applied to human mentality: can you, for instance, observe, sufficiently correctly to forecast consequences, mental characteristics which you do not yourself possess? (Ibid., p. 163)

Here Webb is pointing to the importance of understanding another person on the basis of one's own experience, projecting oneself into the shoes of another through empathising with them. To recast Webb's question, would an observant visitor from Mars be able to grasp human mentality? Would their predictions about the behaviour of human beings, although generally accurate, fall short when particular individuals were encountered? Webb seems to be saying that you have to be able to use your own experience if you really want to understand and predict another's acts. If so, the technology/applied science approach to therapy has shortcomings. We might know that a certain scientific generalisation provides a sound basis for devising a therapeutic technique but not know for sure that its application would work out well with a particular client. This is rather like the forecaster who can predict the climate but not the weather. To be able to predict and control behaviour in general does not mean that you can identify with the experiences of the particular person, who is the subject of prediction, in order to intuit how she will respond.

Put differently, the Martian cannot understood what is in the mind of the human being without sharing his mentality. We know that in everyday life we do not act like scientists. We anticipate accurately the feelings and behaviour of others without having to compute scientific equations. The source of our knowledge must lie elsewhere, and it seems inconceivable that therapy could be practised without it. A diary entry of 1884 is worth quoting at length because the points Webb makes could not be put more elegantly:

> The elements which build up these complex existences which we call feelings, ideas and acts of will, can only be discovered and examined within our own consciousness. By a long involved series of inferences, the conclusion of which recommends itself to our faith by its congruity with all other experience, and by its confirmation through correct anticipation, we assert that these elements exist in other minds. An appreciation of the exact combination of these elements in the thoughts feelings and actions of men can result only from a delicate interchange of an objective and subjective experience. In the appreciation of a thought or feeling no thoroughness of observation will make up for the deficiency in personal experience of the thought or feeling [concerned] ... the possession of a mental quality is necessary to the perception of it. (Ibid., p. 163)

One clear implication of the importance of empathy is that every therapist needs it. Knowledge of an objective kind is not sufficient, although it could well be necessary and applicable. We can indeed predict the climate with a fair degree of accuracy and this is extremely valuable knowledge. It is also possible to justify the application of science without confirmation of empathy. For instance, work with a severely autistic, non-verbal child might yield a good outcome without necessarily knowing what thoughts or feeling the child happens to be having. In this case, we rely on the fact that empirical knowledge is a valuable pointer as to what might be helpful. Technical expertise based on scientific findings really comes into its own when we have a good theoretical understanding of the causes of a problem. However, framing what the problem is for a self-reflective adult who feels stuck and wishes to change is not something for which science can provide an answer. The individual is faced with an existential question about his life as a whole and responsibility for producing a response to this question rests with the person concerned. If technology helps, it is only as a tool to overcome particular obstacles.

Abraham Maslow

By the mid-twentieth century, existentialist philosophers had loaded freedom of choice squarely upon the shoulders of each individual. The authenticity of the choices that shaped a person's life came to be highly valued. A person was expected to choose what she believed would fulfil the meaning she wished her life to have. This could, of course, mean anything from political activism to a life of unrestrained hedonism.

Assuming that a person is honestly striving for authenticity, it implies that he desires to be open to experience and perhaps to throw off prohibitions and ingrained rules to see how a "new face" fits. Abraham Maslow was a key figure whose theories led away from the prevailing emphasis on distress and abnormality (ie., "neurosis") on to what it was possible for a person to become under optimal conditions when basic needs had already been met (Maslow, 1970). In Freud's theory of motivation, the emphasis was on sex and other physiological needs, and "neurosis" resulted when these needs were thwarted. According to Maslow, once basic needs are fulfilled, higher needs come into the ascendance, ones that concern a search for meaning and purpose.

If self-actualisation is recast as an ability to overcome new challenges through an ability to solve problems, we can view it as basic as any other drive in the evolution of human beings. For instance, amongst the hominids, the success of Homo sapiens can be attributed to its ability to solve problems that other hominids could not. The use of fire, sophisticated tools, an ability to survive in different climates, the exploitation of different floras and faunas, all betoken a natural inclination to overcome the difficulties of survival through experimentation (Gamble, 2007). And now, as inbuilt problem-solvers, we need assistance from a therapist only when completely stumped. To have one's endeavours blocked induces a sense of helplessness, and then ultimately hopelessness, when the future offers no glimpse of a way out. There is evidence that hopelessness is associated with a state of depression and risk of suicide (Abramson et al., 2000). Maslow therefore seems to have been right in contending that the human drive to explore, play, experiment, and solve problems had been neglected by previous theorists.

Carl Rogers

Another major figure in humanistic therapy is Carl Rogers. The collection of his autobiographical writings is called *A Way of Being*, a title that accurately encapsulates the fact that the philosophy, values, and personality of the man cannot be divorced from his work as a therapist (Rogers, 1980). At times, he writes as if his peak moments while conducting therapy bring him into touch with a higher realm of consciousness and, indeed, he did acquire in his lifetime the status of a guru. Rogers was brought up in a fundamentalist religious home and reports that "anything I would today regard as a close and communicative interpersonal relationship with another was completely lacking" (ibid., p. 28). He attended a theological seminary before switching his studies to clinical psychology, after which he worked in a child guidance clinic. At this time, in the 1920s and '30s, the clinical psychologist's role was to test, diagnose, and interpret observations, all from a psychoanalytic perspective. As Rogers began to conduct therapy himself, he discovered that this was, for him, "a socially approved way of getting really close to individuals". In contrast to psychoanalytic interpretation, he discovered the value of listening, warmth, and reaching out to others in order to understand them.

Roger's workshops, books and papers subsequently made him into one of the most influential psychologists of the twentieth century. The hallmark of his approach to therapy was indeed "a way of being". To listen and "really hear" what a person was saying seems to have provided as much release and satisfaction for him as it did for his clients. He believed that this kind of communion opened up a person to change and released them from a kind of isolation. He cites as his influences Søren Kierkegaard, Martin Buber, and oriental philosophers, such as Lao-Tze. The principles of his therapeutic style can be summed up as "accurate empathy" (in which the therapist can resonate with what a client deeply feels but can barely articulate), "congruence" (what the therapist feels and is aware of is congruent with what is being communicated) and "non-possessive warmth" (prizing and loving a client without ulterior motive).

Rogers readily admits that he was sometimes unable to practise what he preached with friends, and later in life he was in conflict with his wife over how to reconcile their different needs. With surprising candour, he writes:

> In my experience, I have found that one of the hardest things for me is to care for a person for whatever he or she is, at that time, in the relationship. It is so much easier to care for others for what I think they are, or wish they would be, or feel they should be. (Ibid., p. 85)

Rogers' admission of his difficulty is an example of his honesty and authenticity, not a flaw in his principles. From the standpoint of friendship, Rogers' outlook seems to combine the virtues of a "good and genuine friend" with Christian benevolence. However, Rogers was keen to demonstrate, by means of research, that his style really was helpful. It was not enough simply to argue that his values were intrinsically good. A recent survey of empirical studies backs up his view that therapists who possess the qualities he identified do in fact produce greater benefits for their clients (Castonguay & Beutler, 2006).

Rogers is more open to criticism when he gives the impression that clients, when alone, or in face-to-face contact with their therapists, exist in an existential bubble. In an essay entitled "Do we need 'a' reality?" he concludes that:

> The only reality I can possibly know is the world as I perceive it and experience it at this moment. The only reality you can possibly know is the world as you perceive and experience it at this moment. (Ibid., p. 102)

On the one hand, this must be true; I cannot have your experiences. On the other hand, our experience is so tied up with others and the world that it is artificial to put a circle around it. People do not perceive what is in their mind. Their perceptual experience is determined by what has just happened (in the world or what has just been said) and anticipates what is about to happen. The point Rogers appears to be making is that throughout history there was one reality that the members of a group had to adhere to. Now, in the modern world, there are many realities to choose from. He argues that the belief that there is a "real world" is "a luxury we cannot afford, a myth we dare not maintain" (ibid., p. 104). Each of us has to explore our own realities. This rather overstates the argument for inner realities, as if they exist in a separate realm of the mind. In fact, Rogers makes an about turn when he goes on to suggest that exploring our own reality would enable us "to cope with the reality in which each one of us exists". Rogers therefore seems to be saying that there is a shared reality and one that we are required to cope with.

Consequently, Rogers overdraws the distinction between "my world" and "your world". Moral dilemmas belong to "our world" and the question of personal ownership only becomes clearer when people decide what it is they can legitimately lay claim to as "theirs". The process of maturing as a person is often a matter of staking a position *vis a vis* one's family or society. In other words, although the starting point is always personal experience, the finishing point is usually a clarification of what kind of "self" one wishes to be, and where obligations to the world can be staked out.

Critics have argued that self-actualisation is a selfish philosophy because it focuses on an individual's inner determinants, neglecting the rightful needs of others (Wallach & Wallach, 1983). Clients' family and friends are, of course, often intimately involved in their problem. However, an inner focus does not necessarily imply selfishness. The inner prompting may be a sense of frustration, meaninglessness, or suffering. The person then searches for outer promptings (e.g., the social triggers) for this inner state of mind. There is also no reason to suppose that what one wants or decides will necessarily be selfish. A focus on oneself may point to shame and guilt, not unfulfilled desires which one feels entitled to gratify. Narcissistic individuals have to pay close attention to themselves, in order to see that their own self-absorption is creating difficulties for themselves and others.

The contrast between friendship and a non-directive style of therapy

Not all humanistic therapists adopt a non-directive style but when they do, it is motivated by a desire to respect clients' experiences and their unique striving after meaning. The therapist does not see it as his place to impose values or to give advice that explicitly takes a moral position. Unlike a friend who says, "You must be crazy to do that," or, "I think you're misjudging her," therapists will enquire about other ways their client might view the issue, the person, etc. One of the advantages of friends is that they feel free (or ought to) to speak their mind.

The same openness from a stranger would most likely be resented. In this respect, humanistic therapists see themselves as strangers rather than as friends.

Accordingly, it could be argued that a non-directive style is insufficiently proactive. The therapist does not attempt to formulate for a client what his problem might be, and therefore this style does not capture all that we might wish for when we turn to another for help. For instance, we might want more guidance, or to test out our intuition about how to solve a problem. Are we seeing things straight or have we missed something important? We might want a therapist to act as an advocate or to offer emotional support. A person may not know what it is that would help them to feel authentic and true to his own self. It is not as if the "self" is some inner unchanging core, waiting to be released; it is something made up as one goes along. For this reason, a person often experiments (with drugs, with foreign travel, etc.) in order to allow his experience to determine his sense of self. In a similar way, a person may want direct advice from a therapist. It allows him to be guided towards something that does in fact feel more authentic. In most cases, there is no reason to believe that he would not feel at liberty to reject the new experience if it did not feel right.

A non-directive style is consonant with the values of a liberal democracy in which the individual's right to choose (even obviously stupid acts) is respected. People are allowed to be perverse if that is what they want to be. Perhaps all human beings value self-determination. The old proverb, "You can take a horse to water but you can't make it drink," certainly strikes true as a rule of thumb in therapy. A person needs to persuade themselves of the wisdom of a piece of advice. For this reason, a non-directive approach may be more successful than a directive one, especially when a person is equivocating about making a change.

Taken to an extreme, the non-directive style has been parodied by comedians. The therapist is portrayed as too squeamish to have any kind of influence at all. This hands-off attitude can underestimate the capacity of a client to grasp where a therapist's questioning is inevitably leading. Clients are not so stupid that they cannot gauge what position a therapist takes on a moral issue. Therapy, like friendship, can pursue its objectives when the participants hold strong and opposing positions. Respect is a two-way process, and therapists should be entitled to have their own views considered, even when they are rejected. Therapists rarely impose their opinion, although there are times when a therapist might feel obliged to give strong advice. For example, when a client is regularly being beaten up by his or her partner, most therapists would try to extract them from this situation.

A brief comment on contemporary humanistic therapies

Carl Roger's person-centred therapy is only one of a wide number of humanistic therapies (Schneider & Leitner, 2002). The stress on personal experience links it to phenomenology and existentialism, each of which has shaped a distinctive therapy approach. Some therapies stress the here and now, whether of thought, feeling, or bodily experience. The aim is to empower a client, facilitate self-discovery, and "raise consciousness".

Like all forms of therapy, humanistic therapies have been drawn in by the evaluation ethos of managed mental health care, in order to prove effectiveness and streamline their techniques. This is a path that leads to a specification of "core competencies" and "standards of proficiency", to organise training in accordance with them, and to professionalise therapy through systems of accreditation and regulation so that "unfit" therapists can be prevented from practising. If it succumbs to this trend, humanistic therapy will probably lose values that essentially define it (Murphy, 2011). It would de-emphasise the spontaneous and improvisational nature of the therapy relationship and have a tendency to freeze the practice of psychotherapy in time. As McGivern and Fischer (2012) point out, the twin strategies designed to ensure transparency—monitoring outputs through standardised measures and subjecting therapists to rigorous professional regulation—distort practice and judgement. The service is geared to hitting targets, and practitioners make sure that any personal reflections they record during therapy (their session notes) omit anything that might place them at risk when dealing with a potential allegation of poor practice. In the words of the outgoing president of the American Psychological Association's Society for Humanistic Psychology:

> The huge strategic mistake we humanistic psychologists made was allowing the emancipatory framing that deliberately put the humanistic discourse outside of, alternative to, and critical of medicalized psychology, to become seduced and co-opted by it. (O'Hara, 2009, p. 2)

The humanistic approach and professional ethics

There are limits on genuineness, authenticity, and compassionate love in the context of a professional relationship. The client is kept at a distance by regulating the frequency and timing of appointments. It is easier to terminate a relationship with a client than it is with an old friend. Regard for a client cannot be unconditional, and the relationship genuinely equal, because professional ethics forbid it (see Chapter Eleven). A therapist is advised not to socialise with clients or suggest any kind of joint business arrangement. She is strongly recommended not to divulge details of her own personal life. The prohibition on stepping outside the role of therapist extends to transactions with associates of the client, and also beyond the termination of therapy. It is frowned upon, but not absolutely forbidden, to employ an ex-client in any capacity.

These codes of conduct could of course be challenged but they are designed to protect the therapist as much as the client. A therapist can emulate Rogers' "way of being" but its boundaries have to be explained. Most people now know enough about the social role of a therapist not to need reminding of it. Clients can avail themselves of the benefits of therapy while both parties are protected from unwanted complications.

CHAPTER FOUR

The psychodynamic approach

The theoretical ideas that underlie psychodynamic therapies can be traced to Sigmund Freud and the circle of people surrounding him at the beginning of the twentieth century. Freud's early theory highlighted the role of sexual and aggressive instincts in a person's life and how they could be reconciled with external reality. It was a rational part of the mind (the ego) that mediated this difficult task. It did so by constructing "defense mechanisms" in order to maintain a healthy balance between different forces. The superego was another part of the mind that controlled instinctual urges through guilt.

Freud later changed his original theory. Other major figures (e.g., Carl Jung, Alfred Adler, Otto Rank, Karen Horney, and Melanie Klein) went in different theoretical directions and developed their own forms of psychodynamic therapy. My aim in this chapter is to give a broad-brush account of what I consider to be the essential characteristics of a psychodynamic approach. A survey of the whole field would be an enormous undertaking and so I will focus on the way Freudian ideas were absorbed and became a mainstream therapeutic approach. Psychoanalysis is the most familiar psychodynamic therapy and I will use it for illustration. The term "psychodynamic" is much broader than "psychoanalytic", referring to a variety of techniques and theories.

Compared with psychoanalysis, sessions are spaced less frequently and a course of therapy is shorter. Moreover, psychodynamic therapists do not have to undergo their own training analysis with an approved psychoanalyst in order to qualify to practice.

Embedded in most psychodynamic therapies are the following three assumptions. The first is a carry-over from the philosophy of mind that was current in Freud's day. It conceives of the mind as a kind of enclosed space, and in this space, at conscious and unconscious levels, there are interacting energies, instincts, motives, emotions, ideas, images, etc., that occupy it. Events at the unconscious level have to be inferred from what a client says and from her bodily signs, such as a tense posture, sighs, or a facial expression. The second assumption is that what happens in the mind is largely related to a person's biological nature. For instance, it is assumed that there are a limited number of largely inborn patterns of attachment between a child and its caregivers during early development. There is also an emphasis on the brain as the biological basis of the mind, an assumption that continues to be reflected in attempts by neuroscientists to locate the causes of "mental disorders" in the brain. The importance of biology and physiology was quite explicit in Freud's early thinking. He viewed "psychic energy" (libido) as part of an organic system in which energy was blocked, conserved, or discharged. Although the focus has now shifted onto the social origins of clients' problems, the contribution from social science theory has been limited. This is rather surprising given the number of sociologists who have been attracted to psychoanalytic theory. The third assumption common to psychodynamic therapies is the significance placed upon the relationship between therapist and client. This is a natural consequence of Freud's observation that childhood conflicts and traumas were re-enacted with the therapist. Therapy is conceived as a kind of healing or maturational process taking place through the medium of the relationship.

Sigmund Freud and psychoanalysis

Freud developed his ideas at the latter end of the nineteenth century when people sought treatment for conditions classified by psychiatrists and physicians as nervous diseases or "neuroses". These conditions had no known physical cause although efforts were being made to understand them as illnesses. They were divided into two main types: hysteria and psychasthenia. Hysteria was more common amongst women; the symptoms included a hypersensitivity to ideas and emotions, and sometimes a dulling of sensation to the point of deafness, blindness, insensitivity to pain, and motor paralysis. By contrast, a person with psychasthenia was described as inhibited, indecisive, anxious, obsessive, and, unlike a hysteric, aware that her mind was split between her normal and abnormal experiences. A hysteric was thought to be actively repressing this awareness; for her, her symptoms were "real".

As can be seen, the context of complaint was medical; problems, viewed as illnesses, were defined by doctors. The term "psycho-therapeia" had been introduced earlier, in 1853, and the role of the "psychotherapist" was to diagnose the illness and, where possible, treat the underlying cause. Psychotherapists were doctors by profession.

Freud trained as a physiologist before becoming a physician, and he thought of himself as a scientist. In 1886 he set up a private practice for nervous diseases. A colleague, Josef Breuer, developed the hypothesis that hysteria was caused by an intense emotional experience that the patient had forgotten. Breuer and Freud published a case study of a twenty-one-year-old woman who suffered from paralyses, impaired eyesight, and difficulty keeping her head erect. She was unable to drink in spite of intense thirst. This woman had been caring for a beloved and dying father but, on account of her own illness, she had to give up nursing him. During hypnosis she spoke about her fantasy of being at her father's sickbed, after which she was relieved of her symptoms and resumed her normal life. Freud and Breuer concluded that a patient's symptoms had meaning and could be cured by a disclosure of their unknown significance. Freud later broke away from Breuer, dispensed with hypnosis, and worked out his own techniques for the recall of memories based on free association and dream interpretation. Subsequent archival research has shown that this particular patient was not cured and was actually suffering from tuberculous meningitis (Eysenck, 1985).

For Freud, patients posed a scientific puzzle. The task was to discover the psychological events in their history that had interfered with the expression of their natural instincts. This exploration could take several years. An article entitled "The justification for detaching from neurasthenia a particular syndrome: The anxiety neurosis", published in 1894, illustrates how Freud was thinking at the time (Freud, 1894). His skill in describing what we now call panic attacks, and their associated fears, cannot be faulted. He highlighted an exaggerated perception of future ill-health or other catastrophe, linking the experience of anxiety to a variety of bodily sensations. The features he so ably described form the core of recent theories of panic attacks that are now widely accepted. However, Freud did not look for causes within the surface features of what he observed. He considered sexual inhibition to be the actual origin of panic attacks. He speculated that nervous disease was the outcome of a "damning up" of instinctual energies, which overflowed into unwanted and distressing neurotic illnesses.

Freud illustrated his thesis about the cause of panic attacks with examples such as a young girl's first encounter with sex, unconsummated sexual excitement, anxiety in the newly married, sexual abstinence, giving up masturbation, and the practice of *coitus interruptus*. Essentially, he argued that in "anxiety neurosis" somatic sexual excitation was deflected from the "psychical sphere" into troublesome bodily reactions. As a scientific theory, it has no credibility today. Many of Freud's scientific hypotheses were similarly put forward in a speculative way without any of the necessary experimental checks. One of his contemporaries, the American physician Morton Prince, drawing upon academic psychology, interpreted the phenomena Freud described in ways that resemble present-day accounts of panic (Prince, 1911). All that Freud needed to have done was to apply a little science in a careful and systematic way. As an avowed scientist, he must have been swept along by enthusiasm for his own convictions.

As Freud developed his ideas, his interests went far beyond the complaints of his patients and extended into speculations about culture and the human condition. His influence on art and literature was immense. However, we have to agree with Hans Eysenck's verdict that he was simply too free with his speculations (Eysenck, 1985). Eysenck, though not a therapist himself, saw his mission as inspiring his colleagues to apply the theory and findings of experimental psychology to therapy. He also encouraged them to develop methods that made a difference to a problem *as presented*. At that time, and perhaps even now, many psychoanalysts did not accept that the problem *was* the problem. Freud's legacy includes the comment inevitably directed at a psychologist when her or his job is first made known: "You must be able to read my mind." In other words, anything of importance must lie hidden.

An interview with Freud conducted in Austria in 1930 tells us a great deal about how he viewed himself as a public figure and as a therapist. By then, Freud was over seventy years old. The interview was conducted by a German American, George Viereck, well known for his interviews with famous people: the list includes George Bernard Shaw, Adolf Hitler, Henry Ford, and Albert Einstein (Viereck, 1930, reprinted 1994). I assume that Viereck had a very good memory or else he was able to write in shorthand. I cannot of course vouch for the veracity of the words spoken.

Viereck was clearly in awe of Freud, who does not brush off the fame his interviewer projects on to him:

> Fame comes to us only after we are dead … I have no aspiration to posthumous glory. (Ibid., p. 265)

This sounds disingenuous given that Freud was by this time almost universally famous. When asked about the appeal of reincarnation and immortality, Freud remarks:

> Frankly, no. If one recognises the selfish motives which underlie all human conduct, one has not the slightest desire to return … our life is necessarily a series of compromises, a never-ending struggle between the ego and his environment … all life combines with the desire to maintain itself, an ambivalent desire for its own annihilation. (Ibid.)

Freud had a rather bleak view of the world. When the subject turned to therapy, Freud mentioned that he was "working on a difficult case, disentangling the psychic conflicts of an interesting new patient" (ibid., p. 267). As already noted, Freud saw himself as a scientist, uncovering the causal determinants of the problem (he does not say what it was).

Viereck then asks Freud about self-analysis and how he views his own role:

> The psychoanalyst is like the scapegoat of the Hebrews. Others load their sins upon him. He must exercise his art to the utmost to extricate himself from the burden cast upon him. (Ibid.)

It seems that Freud's words do not mean that he sees himself as a Christ-like figure, expiating the sins of others through self-sacrifice. Rather, his aim is to extricate himself. Nevertheless, he seems to be taking responsibility for other peoples' problems, presumably because he believes that he has the key to unravelling them. He goes on to strongly contradict the idea that he acts out of charity. His following words are perfectly understandable in light of the anti-Semitism (to which he refers) that now surrounds him and will later drive him out of Vienna:

> On the contrary, to understand all is not to forgive all. Psychoanalysis teaches us not only what we may endure, it also teaches us what we must avoid. It tells us what must be exterminated. Tolerance of evil is by no means a corollary of knowledge. (Ibid.)

Viereck has the temerity to ask what his own complexes might be. Freud becomes practical at this point:

> A serious analysis takes at least a year. It may even take two or three years. You are devoting many years of your life to lion-hunting. You have sought, year after year, the outstanding figures of your generation, invariably men older than yourself … the great man is a symbol. Your search is the search of your heart. You are seeking the great man to take the place of the father. It is part of your father complex. (Ibid.)

Viereck privately rejects this interpretation but on what grounds can he do so? The great man has spoken and his protestations could be interpreted as an expression of resistance motivated by the designs of his unconscious mind. Viereck, like any client, or even the stranger who discovers that you are a psychologist, is forced on to the back foot. Interpretations are powerful when they come from the expert of experts. Viereck later wonders if there is any truth in the interpretation. Perhaps there was! According to Wikipedia, which must of course be believed, Viereck's father was reputed to be the son of Kaiser Wilhelm I, born out of wedlock to a German actress (Wikipedia, n.d.).

Freud's reply shows how far he has shifted from being a doctor treating a neurosis. As far as we know, Viereck did not have a neurotic illness. A quest for some inner truth about himself seems to justify spending up to three years of his life searching for it. Freud has no hesitation in throwing out an off-the-cuff interpretation, an enticement to begin the process. However, once engaged with an analyst in the privacy of a consulting room, the material on which interpretation works becomes more concrete because it is based on here-and-now feelings expressed towards the therapist. The therapist has already been set up as an authority figure, somewhat like a parent, and expects that the client will begin to act like the child whose early experiences were full of conflict and trauma. When the client-cum-child expresses those feelings, the therapist-cum-parent can interpret them for what they are: love, hate, regret, disappointment, and so forth. If there is one legacy of Freud's practice that has survived, it is this: the wide acceptance that clients transfer on to a therapist feelings that do not rightfully belong there. In turn, the therapist has come to acknowledge that there are feelings that she cannot but help to transfer onto her client, again sometimes without awareness or without justification.

Once psychoanalysis had begun to broaden its aims, there was a real difficulty in understanding what it was for and how its success could be assessed. As a voyage into the unknown, there was no need to specify a destination. Later on in Viereck's interview, Freud clarifies what an analysis now means to him:

> Psychoanalysis simplifies life. We achieve a new synthesis after analysis. Psychoanalysis reassorts the maze of stray impulses, and tries to wind them around the spool to which they belong. Or to change the metaphor, it supplies the thread that leads a man out of the labyrinth of his own unconscious. (Ibid., p. 269)

It strikes me that Freud, if these really were his words, is a little too handy with his metaphors. The promises he makes are both vague and unverifiable. He still insists in the ensuing discussion that he has discovered the basis of a new science which will continue to change as it searches out and discovers new truths. On one thing he was certain: "I am quite sure that I made no mistake when I emphasised the predominance of the sex instinct." This is a pretty safe wager but hardly the definitive truth.

An early description of psychoanalytic therapy: Eric Berne

Although very dated, Eric Berne's *A Layman's Guide to Psychiatry and Psychoanalysis*, originally titled *The Mind in Action* and first published in 1947, was updated and reissued in 1957. It remained in print until 1971. Berne also achieved best-seller status with his book *Games People Play*

(1964), which is still available. Present-day psychodynamic therapy has moved well beyond Berne's account but the style of working is still in evidence.

Berne reminds his reader that psychoanalysis is always a long process, "one session a week for about three years is probably the minimum for cure" (1957, p. 265). Berne defines cure to mean relieving a patient "of unnecessary doubts, unreasonable guilts, distressing self-reproaches, faulty judgements, and unwise impulses" (ibid., p. 267). The patient is said to come for understanding, not for moral verdicts. Given that guilt and self-reproach smack of morality, it seems likely that clients will receive moral guidance. Perhaps Berne means to say that clients are expected to find their own answers to their dilemmas.

Berne claims that all methods of psychotherapy "depend for their effects on the emotional relationship between the patient and the doctor" (ibid., p. 264). He notes that this emotional relationship is somewhat impeded by the absence of eye contact: "Many patients ... are disturbed just because they cannot see the doctor's face" (i.e., if a client is lying on a couch). Berne explains that the doctor is supposed to keep a "strictly neutral attitude" while also "detecting and pointing out underlying tensions." The therapist must be watchful "lest a misplaced word encourages a self-damaging attitude". So, while striving for neutrality, Berne is suggesting that a therapist has the power to inflict damage (ibid., pp. 267–269).

Berne sums up as follows:

> The analyst remains neutral throughout the treatment, and actually presents himself to the patient as not much more than a guiding voice. As there is no reasonable basis for loving or hating a neutral person, the feelings which swirl around the image of the analyst must not have been aroused by him, but by other people, and the patient, with his permission and supervision, uses the analyst as a scapegoat for tensions he could not relieve on their proper objects. (Ibid., p. 271)

The material for interpretation consists of feelings projected onto the therapist. The rationale is that by gaining insight into transferred feelings (understood to be the residue of earlier events and relationships) a client is freed from the urge to relate to others in self-defeating and essentially irrational ways. The therapy relationship is hard work and may become intensely emotional. It may create dependency on the therapist. Berne stresses that the "very purpose of analysis" is ultimately to take pains to analyse and dissolve "this very bond", thereby leaving the patient free and independent (ibid., p. 270). Present-day psychoanalysts acknowledge the difficulty dissolving the bond of dependency. The British Psychoanalytic Council is not sanguine about leaving the patient in a state of independence. Their ethical code of practice includes the following rule:

> Registrants must nominate two colleagues to hold a list of their patients and supervisees in confidence, in the event of death or an inability to work. The names of these nominees must be lodged with the constituent societies. (BPC, n.d.)

Some psychotherapists go further and include the continuing care of their clients in their will. A friend beyond the grave! (Pope & Vasquez, 2007).

Subsequent developments in the psychodynamic approach

Psychodynamic theory and technique has changed greatly in the past forty years. If there is one common feature, it is a focus on what happens moment by moment in a therapy session. The feelings aroused in the client and in the therapist are interpreted, making it an essentially verbal therapy, even when little is said. The chief events of interest in the relationship are the transference and countertransference. It is assumed that a client will project onto a therapist, or re-enact, the sort of relationships he has had with carers in childhood. The concept of transference and other key concepts, such as resistance, have now been taken up by other schools of therapy, including cognitive behavioural therapy (CBT) (See, for example, Leahy, 2001; Young, Klosko & Weishaar, 2003).

Instead of Berne's "projection-screen" mode of working, there is now much greater emphasis on the interaction between both parties (Karon & Widener, 1995). A therapist still uses the immediate interplay of interpersonal events as they unfold in a session but the therapist becomes an active instrument for change. He is "attuned to", "mirror or match", "hold", and "contain" the client's feelings (Fonagy, 2001; Nolan, 2012). When using these techniques, a therapist has to rely a great deal on interpreting his own emotional responses to a client, managing how he modulates the interaction, using his intuition to produce helpful interpretations.

The terms illness and neurosis are still used. We cannot blame Freud for his medical language or his outdated philosophy of mind because they reflect the assumptions of his day. However, Lomas, a psychodynamic therapist, still talks of "healing" the "illnesses" of his patients (1993, p. 65). What illnesses? Lomas is by no means alone in using medical terminology. Academic researchers still refer to psychopathology as a branch of applied science.

Despite a far greater reliance on empirical studies of infant interactions with their carers, much of psychodynamic theory is speculative. The innovations that have been introduced over the years have come mostly from practitioners working outside academic institutions. Consequently, they have not always been subjected to rigorous examination for their internal logic and supporting evidence. The field is characterised by leaders and followers, with schools bickering between themselves. There are separate professional organisations for each one, and numerous journals that follow a party line.

Since Freud's day, philosophers have introduced completely new conceptions of "mind". These developments have had a huge impact on social science and theories of therapy. The dynamics of change are now no longer seen as exclusively located in internal and private spaces. The metaphor of the mind as a container has lost most of its credibility, even though it still exists as the framework for talking about ourselves in everyday conversation. When applied to therapy, the metaphor conjures up for me a picture of the therapist as a fisherman sitting quietly and unobtrusively on the banks of a stream, dipping a rod and line into the unseen depths of the water (the patient's mind) hoping to fish out some nuggets of dreams, slips of the tongue, and spontaneous fantasies in order to interpret them.

This is not to suggest that important memories and forgotten truths cannot be detected from flimsy associations. However, a therapist has now become a much more active figure, an interlocutor or collaborator, searching for information that belongs as much in the public sphere as in the workings of an inner space. The material for interpretation can be greatly enriched by directing attention to public events in a client's life (currently or in the past), including the thoughts, reactions, and opinions of others. The therapist's own feelings towards a client in a session (the countertransference) remain a primary source of interpretation and explanation. However, it is now accepted that the usefulness of therapy has to be tested in the public world. Insight into the remote childhood causes of a problem may be necessary but therapy has to make a practical difference to the way clients experience their life as lived.

The exchange of ideas between psychodynamic and other approaches has been two-way, with a strong influence from humanistic therapy. Christopher Bollas, an "object relations" theorist, speaks of "how analyst and analysand unconsciously work together to develop new psychic structures". By this he means that they "select narrative and mental objects to bring about inner states in each other". Although they are doing so unconsciously, the client sounds more like an equal participant (Bollas, 1992, pp. 5–6). Peter Lomas (1993) echoes Carl Rogers when he stresses the importance of being authentic, genuine, and spontaneous. He sees limitations in the "creative deprivation" a client must feel when lying on a couch, unable to see the analyst, receiving no response to normal conversational gambits. He believes that the therapist's moral neutrality and restraint on showing warmth can have a detrimental effect on the well-being of both parties. Lomas also rejects the blank screen, neutral stance described by Berne. He feels that a therapist's personality, attitudes, and values are bound to get transmitted to a client. A quotation from one of his own sessions illustrates the point. A client ended it by saying, "I want to stay here all day and drink warm milk" (Lomas, 1993, p. 44). No one has ever said anything quite like that to me during several decades of work as a therapist. Other messages will have got through, but not ones that suggest breastfeeding a baby.

The nature of the client/therapist relationship

In the three approaches I cover, a client's relationship with a psychodynamic therapist is least like friendship. There is great emphasis on separating the roles of therapist and client, and this concern with "boundaries" can be found in the codes of conduct of all professional therapy organisations. This distancing from the client may be related to the fact that Freud was a medical doctor and saw himself as a scientist. A client lying on a couch (although this is no longer a typical) becomes an "object" to be observed rather than an interlocutor. It is the emotional atmosphere generated between client and therapist, rather than a dialogue, that is seen as the crucible for change. This heightens the emotional significance of any variation in routine, such as a client missing an appointment, arriving late, or a therapist taking a holiday. An "emotional bond" is certainly an important feature, as in friendship, but it does not have the openness and even-handedness that exists between friends.

Jefferson Fish, a therapist who trained as a psychoanalyst, explains how this bond can develop. He gives the example of a female client meeting with a male therapist whom she is assured can be trusted with secrets she may have told no one else. The therapist is an intelligent and understanding man who shows interest in her thoughts and feelings, including her sexual feelings and experiences, and he also shows concern for her welfare. As Fish observes, "it sounds a lot like a romantic involvement" (Fish, 1996, p. 48). Of course, the more therapy focuses on these elements (as it often does) the more it encourages such feelings. Interpreted as seduction, Fish finds it quite understandable that the termination of therapy can be a problem for psychoanalysts. "They have created such an interpersonal tangle that it takes a long time to extricate themselves from it" (ibid., p. 50).

Fish now believes that a collaborative relationship is all that is really necessary or desirable in order to solve problems. When the problem is solved, therapy ends naturally. When it is not solved, or is only partially solved, this is openly acknowledged. Paul Wachtel (1977) also feels that therapists should be open about how they influence clients and should foster an atmosphere of collaboration. He contrasts this with the way transference is employed in psychoanalysis:

> For the therapist, then, to use the power that has been transferred to him by virtue of his participation in the role of therapist—to influence the patient not by directing himself to the patient as a rational choosing adult, but by playing upon the childish fears and longings that are evoked by the therapeutic process—would seem to be an abuse of the trust that has been placed in him. (Ibid., p. 281)

One of the risks of the kind of relationship that is generated is therefore to infantilise a client, underestimating a client's capacity (and moral obligation) to act in a responsible and adult manner. When the therapy relationship is conceived as a crucible for changing feelings transferred onto the therapist, it may encourage an acting out of impulsive, childlike emotions. A client who has been given a label of, say, "a borderline personality", is virtually expected to regress to an infantile way of responding.

Clients may, of course, act emotionally towards a therapist in ways that have been determined by earlier damaging relationships. Psychodynamic therapists would argue that they work with the "healthy part" of clients' minds in order to give insight into their impulsive and self-defeating ways of relating. However, there are other ways of working with a legacy of emotional abuse without having it re-enacted in the relationship with a therapist. In my view, this technique may handicap the required level of detachment and reflection necessary to initiate change in the real world. A client's interpersonal difficulties typically occur *outside* the consulting room, and examples of them can provide material for analysis and reflection. Difficulties can also be re-enacted with full emotional involvement in fantasy or role-play, followed by a period of debriefing that leads to suggestions about other ways of resolving a difficulty. The relationship with a therapist can stay at an adult level while interpersonal problems that disturb a client's everyday life remain centre-stage.

A recently reported case study describes how a psychoanalyst changed his technique in this way (Pagano, 2012). The client was a depressed, apathetic, and socially isolated young man with a childhood history of a broken family and an emotionally reserved father. He had a fear of social rejection and had never had a romantic relationship. Following two years of weekly therapy, largely involving the interpretation of feelings and behaviour, the client became frustrated that the therapist was "withholding" and emotionally unavailable. He asked for feedback, practical skills, and homework. He suggested role-rehearsal of a recent interpersonal problem at work. The therapist changed his technique, resulting in an obvious breakthrough in changing the client's behaviour outside the sessions. Therapy continued for another two years, with incremental benefits. In commenting on this case study, the author still felt that the initial two years of work had been necessary to help the client "understand his transference distortions" (Pagano, 2012, p. 222). It seems much more likely to me that had the client received therapy from the outset along more pragmatic lines (for example, schema-focused therapy: Young, Klosko & Weishaar, 2003) the number of sessions would have been closer to twenty than 200. In a follow-up communication, the client said that the breakthrough had come when the therapist became "a real person" rather than a professional.

It has been said that traditional psychoanalysis has some of the features of a religion and, if true, it places it in a different sociological category, one that is certainly not allied to friendship. As a set of beliefs, psychoanalysis has been remarkably resistant to criticism of its underlying assumptions and slow to accept that evidence is needed to demonstrate its benefits. Anyone who is attracted to traditional psychoanalysis is looking for a very special kind of friend indeed—perhaps someone dangerous to know who promises a risk and a challenge. After all, the quarry is something of which they are not even aware, the contents of their unconscious mind.

Psychodynamic therapy in the marketplace

A new kind of pragmatism is bringing about change. Governments (and other funding bodies) will only support treatments for which there is evidence to show that they "work". There is also an expectation that any therapy worth its salt should be able to specify the knowledge and skills a therapist needs to acquire. In relation to psychodynamic therapy in the UK, this task has fallen to Alessandra Lemma and her colleagues (Lemma, Roth & Pilling, 2014). The strategy they adopted was to abstract from a number of manuals of psychodynamic treatments reflecting a range of theoretical traditions. All purported to be examples of "applied psychoanalysis".

The authors therefore decided to ignore the distinction between psychoanalytic and psychodynamic therapy. However, in line with the medical origins of psychoanalysis, Lemma and colleagues retain the terminology of neurotic, borderline, and psychotic types of problem. The focus remains on the inner world of the client and the micro-processes of the therapy relationship. Clients are informed not to expect practical guidance or the alleviation of symptoms because the aim is to understand the unconscious meaning of their complaints. Clients are also warned to expect rather few questions and the occasional long silence. It is stated that strict attention will be given to the boundaries of the relationship, the length and regularity of sessions, the physical surroundings of therapy, and the open acknowledgement (and repair) of therapist errors. The authors' lack of emphasis on the alleviation of a presenting problem is clearly consistent with the aims of psychoanalysis. However, it seems inconsistent with the spirit of showing that psychodynamic therapy "works", given that most forms of evaluation rely on measures of "symptoms".

As a common denominator of various therapy manuals, the approach that Lemma and colleagues have settled upon is likely to include one form of brief psychodynamic psychotherapy which was compared with CBT in a recent randomised control trial (Driessen et al., 2013). In their allotted quota of sessions, the therapists show "a supportive attitude by empathizing and being accepting, committed, active, flexible, clear, definite, patient, and persistent … reducing guilt, shame and isolation, clarifying, confronting, rationalizing, enhancing self-esteem, advising, and modeling" (ibid., p. 1048). This brief form of psychodynamic therapy "recognizes the existence of transference but does not interpret it". Consequently, it is not clear what makes this therapy psychodynamic. It seems worlds apart from a recent article by Lemma (2014) entitled "Off the couch, into the toilet: Exploring the psychic uses of the analyst's toilet". The toilet is apparently "a place where 'dirty' secrets may be excitedly deposited and where perverse fantasies can be fueled and acted out". It is also "the location of the 'toilet-breast'". This sounds like traditional psychoanalysis, bearing little resemblance to the methods employed by Driessen and colleagues.

In a search of the literature describing manualised psychodynamic therapy, Blagys and Hilsenroth (2000) identified seven features that reliably distinguished it from CBT. These were an exploration of clients' emotions, exploring why clients avoid talking about emotional issues (resistance), identifying recurring themes and patterns in problems, discussing the residue of early childhood attachments, a focus on interpersonal relationships (and on the therapy relationship in particular), and encouraging clients to discuss their fantasy lives.

While not identifying myself as a psychodynamic therapist, the therapy I practise could include any or all of these elements. This may reflect the way that the field has matured into a way of working that borrows from any tradition that seems to offer worthwhile ideas and techniques.

CHAPTER FIVE

Applied science/technology

This chapter discusses the values and techniques of those professionals who place their faith in science. They are also keen to show that their methods actually produce results. On this basis they can anticipate with some confidence that therapy will benefit a client. Broadly speaking, there are two kinds of scientific rationale, each dependent on the other. The first is to take account of scientific theory, chiefly in the form of principles or generalisations drawn from academic research in psychology that are widely accepted to be valid. It would indeed be very surprising if 150 years of psychology and social science had not yielded some useful knowledge to guide a technology for changing human behaviour. The second rationale is to promote therapy techniques that have been experimentally evaluated and shown to produce benefits for clients. In the early history of therapy, evidence for benefit was inferred from detailed case studies. Although work of this type is still being published, evidence for therapy effectiveness is largely sought from the results of randomised control trials (RCTs), a form of evaluation borrowed from medicine. For instance, the beneficial effects of mindfulness (a technique modelled on oriental meditation) have been evaluated experimentally in much the same way as a new medication.

Academic researchers are interested in the process of therapy as well as its benefits, in other words, in how change comes about. Process research can help pinpoint principles of good practice, and also the skills and personality characteristics that differentiate therapists who get good or poor results (Castonguay & Beutler, 2006). An understanding of the therapy process is relevant for all approaches, not just a technical one. Carl Rogers' contribution to research was not so much on effective *techniques* but on the qualities of effective *therapists*. He was one of the first to record therapy sessions and analyse transcripts of the interaction. For him, it was the style of relating to a client that was important, not a prescribed solution to a specific problem. However, in this chapter I will take applied science in the narrower sense to mean developing technical solutions to identified problems.

For a technical therapist, the removal or amelioration of a problem is the chief criterion of success. For this reason, effectiveness has to be given a precise meaning; it is an essential component of the very definition of a technical therapy. We have already seen that a humanistic therapist highlights a personal style of relating, partly because this style is valued in itself and partly because it is believed to be helpful in a general sense. For a psychodynamic therapist, the success of therapy is not so much determined by the removal of a problem as by success in addressing underlying causes.

A technical therapist would prefer that a successful intervention "works" for specific causal reasons, even when these have not yet been fully understood. It is assumed that future research will help to reveal them. A proven effect on a specific problem is essential to the branding of a technical therapy. In essence, therapy is purchased because it delivers its advertised product. From a sociological standpoint, the process is one of rationalisation (Ritzer, 1993). When a social practice such as therapy is rationalised, a set of logically consistent rules is substituted for what was formerly done in a rather messy, traditional way. It's assumed that traditional practices are intuitive, subjective and frequently illogical. In the new rational approach, a task is broken down into its smallest constituents and the single most efficient method for their completion is devised. The aim is to make the whole process predictable and controllable. It is monitored for quality by measuring performance on each component task.

The applied science/technology approach is therefore rather prosaic, aiming to remove a problem in the most efficient way possible. For certain problems, this style of working has much to recommend it. However, it does not encourage an open-ended examination of the way a client is leading his life, nor is it an attempt to deal with a client's conflicts, confusion, or alienation. In its pragmatic way, the goals of therapy are clearly defined and there are unambiguous criteria for what counts as "improvement". Clients are usually assigned a psychiatric diagnosis and an improvement typically means a reduction of "symptoms". This need not be the only way to classify a problem within a technical approach because it is not beyond the wit of researchers to produce alternative definitions of problems and their resolution. For instance, there are rather obvious indicators of improvement for clients who are overweight or unable to sleep. However, these and other problems have complex causes, and it is not so easy to define and measure what they are.

Technical therapies have a variety of theoretical rationales, values, and philosophies. By choosing a goal for therapy, and a way of reaching it, a technical therapist has already made a moral choice about how best to resolve a problem. In offering a service with a clearly defined aim, it is assumed that a therapist possesses the specialist knowledge required to produce change. A client may begin by working towards fairly concrete goals but these are often the first steps towards broader changes that could have a major impact on many aspects of a client's life. Even small and planned changes can set in motion a chain of events with consequences that were not foreseen. For example, learning to be more assertive could have a profound effect on many areas of a person's life. Therapists who use techniques to help a client reach a specific goal would not deny this but they are modest enough not to expect it. They focus on what they know they can achieve. It is hoped that the long-term effects will be beneficial but this cannot be guaranteed. Clients may misunderstand this approach if they believe that the "removal" of a problem is like having a tooth extracted by a dentist. Psychological change is not simply a matter of preferring one thing, or state of being, over another. Just to engage in the *process* of making a change can carry with it a message about *how* to live, quite apart from the specific "goods" it is designed to yield (Smith, 2009).

Science feeds into technical therapies in many guises. In order to illustrate the general approach, I will focus on the way that theories of learning have inspired the creation of new techniques. The sense in which I am using the word "technique" is not just a matter of following the rules that underlie a particular method. Most therapies follow rules of this kind. To qualify as a technique, a method of therapy should also be linked to theory and specialised knowledge.

Scientists have discovered a great deal about how human beings function as organisms and so it is quite credible to suppose that some problems can be traced to "design faults" that can be corrected by re-education or reskilling. People are not built to cope well with traumatic events, and they seem to suffer from problems that are not found in other primates. This may reflect the capacity of human beings to make connections between unrelated and sometimes purely imaginary events. An appreciation of time also means that future events are brought forward into the present in the way they are not in other animals. Aside from these uniquely human processes, there are likely to be parallels between the causes of problematic behaviour in animals and humans. It is not unreasonable to suppose that techniques can be devised on the basis of psychological processes that are valid across species.

Historical context

Therapists who saw themselves as applied scientists first began to make an impact in the 1940s and '50s. They became serious competitors to psychoanalysts who, for the most part, they roundly criticised. The first significant school was known as behaviour therapy, and later, with an infusion from cognitive psychology, it became known as cognitive behavioural therapy or CBT. Initially, the approach drew on theories of learning devised by behavioural psychologists, but the philosophy of behaviourism came under increasing attack from cognitivists who were more willing to speculate about what was going inside the mind. The early forms of therapy loosely based on cognitive science remain today as distinct brands known as rational emotive behaviour therapy and cognitive therapy. However, for the most part, behavioural and cognitive techniques have amalgamated as CBT.

The two major historical figures in theories of learning were Ivan Pavlov and B. F. Skinner. Pavlov studied associative (otherwise known as classical) conditioning, and Skinner studied how habits were learned when new responses led to biologically important consequences (such as food), otherwise known as operant conditioning or instrumental learning. Nearly all of the experimental work that influenced behaviour therapy was conducted with animals. Pavlov's theories were applied early on, from the 1920s, to the acquisition and removal of fears in children. It is perhaps common sense that fear can be learned by an association between events. For instance, a child encountering a ferocious dog in a park might develop a fear of dogs after a single experience of this nature. In many cases, learned fears decline spontaneously but they can also grow over time, especially in a child with a nervous disposition. A technique in which a fearful child is re-acquainted with dogs in a carefully controlled manner often eliminates the problem. These methods were first investigated by Mary Cover Jones (1924).

When first introduced, critics of behaviour therapy attacked it for being mechanistic, especially as much of the theory was developed from the study of animal behaviour. However, it could be argued that all science is mechanistic, and so the criticism may have been lent support by the belief that humans were being treated like animals and without their consent. Most people are happy to consent to mechanistically inspired medicine (often first tested on animals) but when it comes to psychological problems they may feel that anything smacking of mechanism undermines their powers of self-determination. Academic psychologists would probably argue that self-determined behaviour is simply more complex than animal behaviour but does not require special causal principles, such as free will, to explain it. In any case, although we choose to act in different ways, the acquisition of a skill, such as playing the piano or speaking a foreign language, requires immersion in a learning environment and devotion to a set of exercises. We may decide to learn (however mysteriously that impulse comes about) but we cannot decide to be skilful without systematic practice.

It is true that some behavioural techniques have been applied crudely and mechanistically in the past, but any therapy technique can be applied in this way, including humanistic or psychodynamic therapy delivered in the wrong hands. Clients who opt for CBT are given a rationale for the process they are entering into. Techniques are explained and not imposed. Technical therapists share the values of humanistic therapists, such as a belief in genuineness, empathy, warmth, and the desirability of increasing a client's autonomy, even though their efforts to bring about change are more pragmatic.

Andrew Salter: An early exponent of a technical therapy

By way of illustrating the ethos and values of the applied science approach to therapy, I will use the example of Andrew Salter, a psychologist working in New York in the 1940s. His name is little known and he is rarely counted as one of the many figures who are credited with being the founder of CBT. I have chosen to discuss him because he did at least precede the other founders, and he was an early pioneer of a pragmatic application of Pavlovian conditioning theory. Salter's attitude to his clients and his manner of tackling their problems in many ways epitomises a technical approach. His writing style is flamboyant and hyperbolic but for this reason it accentuates the nature of the issues surrounding the definition of a technical therapy. With hindsight, his language could be judged as too forthright. However, Salter was expressing a minority opinion at the time, and his voice was pushing to be heard against a loud chorus issuing from a congregation of psychodynamic therapists.

Salter developed assertiveness therapy, now widely available as a form of interpersonal skills training in educational settings. The dust jacket of the British edition of his 1949 book *Conditioned Reflex Therapy: The Direct Approach to the Reconstruction of Personality* carries the words of H. G. Wells: "The destruction of psychoanalysis is conclusive" (Salter, 1951). However, like the early Freud, Salter saw himself as applying a branch of science with roots in neurology and physiology. He believed that psychotherapy could contribute to world peace by changing inhibited persons, full of hatreds, into persons whose excitatory and inhibitory processes were in balance, "for only the man whose feelings and whose gut are well fed can afford to love his neighbor" (ibid., p. 320). His sentiments appear to have been shaped by recent use of the atomic bomb and the slaughter of the Second World War. He had a folksy and engaging style of writing:

> We are therapists, mechanics if you please, and the theory we want is the theory that leads us to what to do to change the material we work with ... We are not especially concerned with giving the individual stratified knowledge of his past—called "probing". What concerns us is giving him reflex knowledge for his future—called "habits". When the sewage of society gives persons emotional typhoid, they need psychotherapy. (Ibid., pp. 316–317)

For Salter, one of the chief causes of psychological problems was excessive inhibition. He was not concerned with how clients acquired their inhibitions but in his dealings with them he advocated that every question should receive a clear answer, no matter how foolish the question may appear to be. This was to dispense with reason and knowledge, rather than to use it for change. The grounds for this advice were substantiated by later laboratory research into conditioning and learning (Kirsch et al., 2004). What people believe about a learning task, such as what they expect to have to learn and what they imagine its consequences to be, strongly determine whether any learning takes place at all. New learning is superimposed on old learning. People who firmly hold the view that self-sacrifice in the service of others is an important ethical principle may be unwilling to engage with the goals of assertiveness therapy unless their objections to acting differently can be satisfactorily answered.

Salter's aim was to arrange for new emotional experiences through what the person did. What was new about this at the time was his emphasis on action. If a woman was unhappy with her husband, he might suggest divorce (ibid., p 146). He had little time for the backward searching of psychoanalysis:

> It is always easier to look a thousand years back than a minute ahead ... A person may have to change his occupation, or tell off his brother or his mother or father, or solve any of the other problems that make up life. (Ibid., p. 152)

Salter accepted that new emotional habits required practice: "The person who defends his rights with waiters, is strengthening himself for future encounters with his employer and with his mother-in-law" (ibid., p. 154). He suggested that "therapy must be conducted in an atmosphere of optimism and good cheer", but this did not mean "synthetic optimism or platitudinous reassurance". His objective was "to get the individual to do the correct thing by himself" (ibid., p. 158). The "correct thing" is meant in the sense of a moral judgement about what would enhance the quality of a person's life in a general sense.

For all its hyperbole, Salter's basic message has been transmitted to a wide swathe of therapists and is in keeping with some contemporary cultural values. We live in a society in which a person is told: Express yourself! Nevertheless, the problems that make up life, as Salter called them, do not always have single or straightforward answers, and he did of course recognise this.

CBT, of which Salter's work was a precursor, has burgeoned into a mainstream approach that has now been taken up across the world. It is probably the dominant school. Its pragmatic, common-sense philosophy may be easily absorbed by different cultural traditions. Major figures in its development were Albert Ellis, Joseph Wolpe, Arnold Lazarus, and Aaron Beck, amongst many others. Stanley Rachman, himself a major contributor to theory, research, and practice in the field, has written an account of the development of CBT (Rachman, 2015). I will not supply details of current techniques because my concern is with the values and philosophies that underlie CBT and other technical therapies. I will take CBT as representative of a technical frame of mind.

Attitude towards the client

In common with any professional service, a technical solution to a problem is offered on the basis of a contract drawn up between rational adults. A client might view her therapist through distorting lenses but this will be seen as getting in the way of business, rather than the business itself. The contracted service is usually conducted in a warm and friendly manner but the relationship is not seen as the means by which change is produced. The contract specifies what therapy is for, how long it is expected to last, and what criteria define its success. The participants know where they stand, and the client's chief disadvantage is that she has to trust that the therapist possesses the expertise that is necessary to help them. The therapy relationship is assumed to be an exclusive one, by which I mean that a client does not shop around after contracting the service. This would also be the expectation of a lawyer and perhaps even a school of motoring. A client is doomed to be confused if advice is taken from several sources at the same time. It would become very difficult to assess progress if a client were initiating other interventions at the same time directed towards similar ends.

The service is provided on the basis of following scientific principles or consists of techniques that have a good track record for reliably producing benefit. To the client, a technique may come across as applied common sense, and this is more or less what it is in many cases. Information about the technique in the form of a leaflet or book is usually provided. When a client does not fully comprehend the rationale, she may be reassured that it is worth applying because it is known to yield good results with the kind of problem she is troubled by.

Techniques employed to deal with a specific problem are also expected to have wider beneficial consequences and help a client to make the most of life's opportunities. For instance, to become more socially confident could bring significant rewards. Some therapists describe themselves as life coaches or experts in problem-solving. The client is assumed to be fundamentally rational even though she may behave irrationally. A breakdown in the therapy contract takes on the same character as a dispute with one's car mechanic. The expected service has not been delivered.

Technical therapies and "mental health"

A technical approach to therapy can be delivered without reference to mental health or psychiatric disorder. However, at present the provision of technical therapy cannot easily be disentangled from the prevailing ideology of mental illness. Governments and other health providers prefer to fund therapies that are known to be "effective", and they tend to assume that this means an improvement in mental health. In order to demonstrate effectiveness, there is a considerable reliance on systematic evaluation. The difficulty here is in deciding what therapy produces. How can its personal and social value be measured? Take, for instance, this definition of psychotherapy in the *Encyclopedia of Human Behavior:*

> Psychotherapy, generally defined, is any form of treatment for mental illnesses, behavioral and/or other emotional problems, in which a trained person establishes a professional relationship with a client for the purpose of removing, modifying, or reducing existing symptoms and/or behavior problems, and of promoting personality growth and development. (Pusch, Dobson & O'Brien, 2012, p. 240)

As can be seen, this all-encompassing definition sits on the fence on all of the crucial questions. If an effective therapy is one that cures mental illness, an evaluation would measure outcome in terms of a reduction of illness. If it is seen as solving an emotional or behavioural problem, the relevant measure would be problem resolution. If it promotes personality growth, who would know exactly how to measure this?

No matter how effectiveness is defined, a therapy that calls itself a technology has to say what it produces. As we can see from the definition of psychotherapy just quoted, the concept of mental illness is very influential. If accepted as valid, effectiveness means a reduction of psychiatric symptoms. It is now common for funding agencies to require therapists to administer questionnaires that ask about signs of emotional distress understood as medical conditions (anxious or depressed mood, etc.). When technical therapy is interpreted as a form of problem-solving, the imposition of illness criteria to measure effectiveness is bound to have a distorting effect on what is being supplied as the service (see the following chapters for a discussion of this point).

What therapy is it "rational" to offer?

Therapy has to be attentive to a client's wishes, otherwise the client leaves. The philosopher, Edward Erwin, has attempted to specify the grounds upon which it is rational to offer therapy (Erwin, 1997). He argues that it should not be coercive and should aim to be of benefit. However, he says there will be those people who simply wish to feel better and do not know what would make a difference. They will seek guidance about goals and methods. Therapists cannot take a neutral position in this case (if they ever do). Then there will be people who change what they wish for in the light of information conveyed at the beginning of therapy or as a result of alterations in their attitudes or behaviour brought about by therapy itself. What is rational at one stage may not be rational at another.

Erwin considers whether the benefits of therapy could be judged in terms of what it is rational to wish for, which is, in essence to achieve something "good" or to remove something "bad", taking into account logic and any relevant evidence about the best means of obtaining the desired result. Erwin believes that a decision about benefits could be decided rationally without regard to moral questions. However, it is difficult to see how this could be the case because a client might disagree with a therapist's moral values or standards of rationality, and vice versa. It seems that benefit could only be decided on a relatively rational basis. Erwin sets out his own criteria for judging likely benefit as follows. He discounts a client's expressed wishes only when (a) they are based on faulty logic or incorrect information, (b) the wishes are "incoherent", that is, they are impossible to satisfy jointly, (c) their intended effects are futile or harmful, (d) they are "neurotic", in the sense that they are unlikely to produce the satisfaction desired.

These rational considerations do undoubtedly enter into many therapy decisions, whatever approach is employed. Erwin does not see a problem in a therapist influencing a client about desirable aims. In fact, clients often seek advice about what it is rational to wish for, in which case there is a joint negotiation to decide goals and methods. Therapists are very unlikely to endorse goals that are unachievable or, in their judgement, likely to be detrimental to a client's overall welfare.

Applied science and friendship

A technical therapy need not lack the features of friendship that I consider to be essential. This depends partly on how a service is set up. In practice, the commitment to a client is usually more than the offer of a technical fix. It includes an honest and empathic assessment of a client's life circumstances that goes beyond what is reported as "the presenting problem". This is not always done thoroughly, especially when an offer of therapy is conditional on receiving a psychiatric diagnosis followed by a strictly time-limited and rather inflexible set of procedures. To omit a comprehensive assessment and formulation of the circumstances surrounding a client's problem is, in my view, a false economy. There may be matters which, if not attended to, will scupper any hope of obtaining the hoped-for benefits.

Ethical guidelines for technical therapies are essentially the same as for any other type of help. As already noted, a technical approach prefers to have clarity about goals. In some cases, clients are confused, disorganised, and changeable, and therefore unable to be clear about what they want. When the adult nature of a contract cannot be sustained, the technical therapist is somewhat at a loss. In other words, clients who are not motivated to follow techniques, who live chaotic lives, or who fail to attend appointments, create difficulty. It will come as no surprise that technical solutions have been devised to cope with these eventualities. Procedural rules are adopted when behaviour occurs that, for most professionals who offer a service, would be regarded as intolerable.

One well-known therapist and researcher has called these difficulties "therapy-interfering behaviours" (Linehan, 1993). If a therapist responded to a client's unreasonable behaviour with, say, irritation or retaliation, as well he might with a friend, the client would simply leave therapy and feel let down. Linehan's therapy therefore incorporates "fail-safe techniques". For instance, a therapist suspends his spontaneous emotional reaction and manages the situation by role-playing a helpful professional response. Presumably, this technical strategy contrasts with how a humanistic therapist would handle the same difficulties, that is, by finding a way to convey what he genuinely feels. Instead, the ethics of a technical therapist are utilitarian rather than based on principles of honesty or genuineness.

Difficulty defining an end-product of therapy

The lack of an obvious therapy outcome is unsatisfactory for the agencies that pay for it. They would prefer a guaranteed result with a price tag attached. Otherwise, therapy could be seen as a prescription with a vague rationale and an uncertain promise of relief. (Individual consumers can, of course, choose to spend their money in this way). In order to appreciate the difficulty of evaluating the outcome of therapy, consider the following three vignettes describing clients I have worked with. In each case "symptom reduction" would not do justice to the goals of therapy. In fact, it would be difficult to supply any definition of the aims of therapy that lent itself to a purely technical approach.

In my first example, a woman presented with extreme distress over the accidental death of a close friend of her husband. She was in a state of acute grief. Her husband, who idolised her, was unaware of the fact that his wife had been having a long-standing affair with his friend. Under these circumstances, I did not consider it my role to advise my client about how to handle this situation. Her distress was in large part created by a moral dilemma of her own making. However, she needed someone with whom she could reflect on her circumstances. She had no treatable disorder unless her grief was judged to be excessively prolonged. A therapist was more likely to be a dispassionate sounding board than one of her friends in these circumstances and, in fact, she had no one else to turn to. The woman's personal suffering resulted from the deceased individual being her lover, and from a welter of concomitant emotions. From a mental health perspective, this was not a "real" psychological problem because it did not fit any diagnostic category. However, how many cases of depression would not be "real mental health problems" if a client's circumstances were thoroughly investigated?

My second client was a freedom fighter in another country who had failed to carry out an operation which would have led to the death of some policemen. He became deeply depressed, questioning his motives, values, and commitment to the cause. His family, unaware of the circumstances, had him referred to a psychiatrist (in his own country) who was also ignorant of these events in his life. His condition was diagnosed as bipolar mood disorder and he was prescribed lithium medication. It was only in the relative safety of another country, in strictly confidential circumstances, that he was able to relate his story. I was also able to refer him to a psychiatrist who I knew would be sympathetic to his predicament, and with whom he could discuss his previous psychiatric treatment. Once again, it might be objected that this client's problem was entirely untypical of mental illness, despite the fact that he had been diagnosed and treated for a mental illness. The true precipitants of his distress could not, of course, be revealed for political reasons. However, even this man's problem is not really that unusual. An acute conflict may arise because certain facts have to be kept secret, in the home or in the workplace. Rivalries, jealousies, guilt, envy, secret liaisons, unspeakable hatreds, and the like, are not uncommon as causes of suffering.

My last example is in some ways more straightforward. My client had been referred by his employer who was concerned about his occasionally erratic performance. His job was a highly skilled one and his employer did not want to lose him. It became apparent that he experienced a fluctuating mood that was largely unrelated to external circumstances. In fact, he satisfied all the psychiatric criteria for a bipolar mood disorder but to a degree that placed him on the borders of a tolerable degree of mood variation. With my help, he learned psychological strategies that helped him to manage his fluctuating mood. His dilemma was how to convey this situation to his wife, who was somewhat perplexed by her husband's behaviour (and they had only recently married). My client felt that his problem did not warrant referral to a psychiatrist, which would probably have led to an "official diagnosis" and the prescription of medication. He suspected that this course of action would come as a shock to his wife and possibly to his employer as well. In a joint interview with his wife, we laid out a previously agreed position to explain matters as truthfully as we could. The news that her husband expressed the features of bipolar disorder was difficult for her to assimilate but the meeting had a productive outcome. She accepted her husband's position that this was a problem they could both learn to live with.

This vignetter appears to give grounds for assigning my client's problem to a mental illness, thereby satisfying a funding agency that he qualified for a service. He demonstrated the features of bipolar mood disorder, although not to a degree that he could not cope with his job. However, his chief psychological problem, apart from managing his mood, was how to explain his somewhat erratic behaviour to his new wife, and whether or not to announce to the world that he had a psychiatric illness. His problem was not simply his mood swings but the way he presented himself in public. By labelling himself as someone with a disorder, he could negotiate the manner in which he explained himself to his wife and to his employer without going the full distance of seeking the services of a psychiatrist. In his case, a predisposing vulnerability became critical in conjunction with his need to perform well in his job and marriage. A narrow focus on symptoms of distress would have had the effect of concealing the moral context in which the problem arose.

In the next chapter, I consider how therapy can be subsumed within "relationship science". The aim is to rationalise therapy by breaking it down into a set of component skills and to research which ones are needed to ensure therapeutic success.

CHAPTER SIX

Can we compare different approaches to therapy?

The simple answer to this question is "yes". A large amount of research has been devoted towards this end. My purpose is to ask whether it makes sense to compare therapies and to question the logic of the exercise. It may appear obvious that effectiveness can be defined in such a way that it can be applied across different schools of therapy. However, it is only relatively recently that this assumption has seemed reasonable. Faith in it has three allied sources. The first is the idea that the absence of mental well-being (let's call it suffering) is a kind of illness or disorder. This allows success or failure in each therapy to be defined in the same manner. The second source of faith, dating approximately to the 1980s, is the belief that diagnostic classification schemes can give an adequate definition of disorder, thereby allowing the amount of suffering to be quantified. For example, the third edition of the *Diagnostic and Statistical Manual* of the American Psychiatric Association (1980) abandoned some of its earlier psychodynamic tenets and embraced a theory-light description of some common problems (Mayes & Horwitz, 2005). It then became possible, with checklists and arbitrary criteria, to say whether a person did or did not have a particular "disorder", and also to measure the severity of her "illness". Epidemiologists and researchers could then go about their business more efficiently, to some extent hiding the fact that the definitions were conventional and pseudo-medical. The third source of faith comes from an acceptance of the idea that methods of research from medicine that are used to compare one treatment with another can be transferred with equal plausibility to psychological therapy. Thus, the randomised control trial (RCT) has become the gold standard for how to evaluate effectiveness (Chambless & Ollendick, 2001).

In my distant recall of the state of evaluation in the 1970s, few researchers contemplated making comparisons between radically different types of therapy. For instance, a client taken on for behaviour therapy would not have been the sort of client thought suitable for psychoanalysis, and vice versa. The objectives of each therapy were understood to be quite different, setting aside the amount of time needed to achieve them. Furthermore, "effectiveness" did not have an agreed definition because psychoanalysts at that time believed in symptom substitution. In other words, a behaviour therapist's claim to have eliminated a problem (for example, an irrational fear) would have been met by the counter-argument that the underlying causes (unconscious) had not been dealt with. It was believed that new symptoms would arise in their place. As soon as members of each of these schools could agree that their purpose was to treat psychiatric disorders, one of the requirements for employing the RCT method had been fulfilled. Psychodynamic therapy could then enter the race to prove its worth against other forms of therapy. By the 1980s, watered down versions of earlier psychoanalytic prototypes had developed, with a revised understanding of what they were setting out to achieve.

My work as an academic researcher has included conducting several RCTs. Under some circumstances, a RCT is very informative. I am limiting the following remarks to RCTs that compare therapy methods, especially when the latter consist of a combination of interventions. For instance, a client might be taking a medication as well as receiving a package of techniques, each of which has a different purpose. Aside from the complexity of what is being offered, clients themselves may engage with their social environment in entirely new ways over the course of their therapy. Clients might have changed their work, their intimate relationships, or moved address. It is stretching a point to call an experimental evaluation of this nature "controlled". The meaning of control in the context of a RCT is to deliver a therapy method (e.g., cognitive therapy or psychodynamic therapy) in a carefully specified manner, with attention given to equating the length of therapy, the level of therapists' skills, the allegiance they feel towards their method of working, plus other relevant considerations. It is assumed that the positive or negative effect of all extraneous events that happen coincidentally will balance out between the groups of clients being compared. This cannot be guaranteed because changes arising out of therapy could increase the likelihood of these "coincidental" events happening at all. The reality is that there are so many unquantifiable influences that could have a bearing on the outcome of therapy that any interpretation of the results is necessarily speculative. So much has been done of a varied nature, and so much may have happened to a client, that pinpointing the key causal influences is extraordinarily difficult. Bear in mind that the statistical model describing the relationship between all the variables that the researcher has thought to include is intended to be a general one, representing, as far as possible, all of the clients who have taken part in a trial. Moreover, the statistical model is an attempt to represent a dynamic interaction between two or more people over an extended period of time when many of the relevant causal influences have not been quantified.

At its simplest, a RCT involves the following procedures:

1. Identifying a group of clients who share the same problem,
2. Dividing them at random into one group given one method of treatment and another group given a different treatment (or no treatment at all),
3. Measuring the problem in a standard way before and after therapy,
4. Conducting a statistical analysis to compare the amount of change produced by each therapy,
5. Drawing conclusions such as treatment A is as effective as (or no more effective than) treatment B with respect to measures X, Y, and Z.

Benefits are measured shortly after therapy is complete and usually later on when progress is reassessed after, say, six months or a year. Effectiveness is typically measured in terms of degree of disorder (that is, the presence or amount of a type of symptom) but research evaluators typically hedge their bets by including measures of a client's quality of life. These supplementary measures have been called "non-disorder specific" to distinguish them from the main "disorder-specific" measures. Consequently, the results of a RCT consist of a profile of different benefits, allowing a researcher, if so inclined, to pick and choose amongst them to demonstrate effectiveness.

There are numerous obstacles to carrying out a good RCT, and there is no need to spell them out here. It only needs to be said that all unwanted sources of variation in the outcome measures have to be minimised in order for the statistical analysis to give a clear indication of the result. This is achieved by selecting clients with a "standard" problem, by using reliable measures that have the potential to capture change in all of the trial participants, and by routinizing the treatment and delivering it in a standard way. The fact that a RCT does not necessarily resemble the way that therapy is normally conducted may not be of concern if the results reveal something interesting or unexpected. However, these artificially created conditions are sometimes viewed as the optimal form of therapy because close attention has been paid to standardisation and "scientific validation". In other words, "ordinary therapy" may be viewed as inferior because therapists are, in this case, using their own "intuitions" (Lilienfeld et al., 2013).

My criticism of the reasoning supporting RCT evaluations can be summed up as follows:

1. The disorder concept does not stand up to examination. It is best regarded as an element of a mythology or ideology.
2. Without the support of the disorder concept, the rationale for conducting RCTs to evaluate therapy is weak. The resolution of a client's problem (i.e., what counts for her or him as a good outcome) may differ from one client to another. In fact, the desirability of a particular outcome is often something about which scientific reasoning has nothing to say at all. It may reflect clients' opportunities, resources, constrained choices, personal values, and sometimes just their search for a "meaning in life".
3. As the last point implies, the nature of a client's problem can be highly individual. Perhaps it is best to admit that life is an experiment, and that being wise after the event is the norm. In other words, therapy is an experiment as well. We intend it to contribute to our general happiness without knowing that it actually will.
4. The focus on "disorder" carries the implication that it is not necessary to consider the total context of a client's difficulties. Disorders are usually thought to have internal rather than external (environmental) causes. There are no grounds for assuming that internal

causation is, in fact, any more important than external. Both have to be given consideration.

5. To use the results of a RCT to guide a therapist's decision-making is not the only way to ensure that therapists think "scientifically" or self-critically about a client's problem (Hallam, 2013a). There is also a long tradition of systematic single case evaluation that is sensitive to the causes of clients' problems (McLeod, 2010).
6. A list of "empirically proven therapies" is of limited value to a therapist or client. Clients may not know what they want or need when they begin therapy, and they are not, therefore, in a position to know how to choose. In any case, a proven therapy for a given disorder carries only a reasonable prospect of a good outcome (Barlow, Allen & Choate, 2004). The benefit is often very modest. Furthermore, a proven therapy is of little help in the hands of an incompetent therapist.

Some inferences that have been drawn from the results of RCTs

It is now common to publish summaries of the results of RCTs using a statistical method called meta-analysis. This method uses estimates of benefit across studies and averages them even though the studies have employed different measures of effectiveness. It is usual in a meta-analysis to examine how the characteristics of the participants in the various studies, such as their age, gender, socioeconomic circumstances, or presence of other "disorders", influence the results. Setting aside my reservations about the value of RCTs in the first place, the following is a consensus of current opinion.

1. Clients benefit from therapy when they are compared with clients who have not received it (Smith, Glass & Miller, 1980; Lambert & Ogles, 2004; Wampold, 2001).
2. Comparisons between types of therapy (even markedly different ones such as psychodynamic therapy, CBT, or medication) typically produce a null result, that is, no differential advantage for one method over another. This result was predicted by Saul Rosenzweig (1936) and has mostly been confirmed (See, for example, Luborsky, Singer & Luborsky, 1975; Wampold, 2001). Rosenzweig referred to the equivalent effectiveness of different types of therapy as the Dodo bird effect, borrowing his quotation from an episode depicting a race

in Lewis Carroll's *Alice in Wonderland*: "Everybody has won, and all must have prizes."

3. With regard to the amount of benefit clients receive, this obviously varies a great deal between clients, with a small minority getting worse. Attempts to predict the causes of variation in outcome have found that around forty per cent of variation cannot be predicted from any of the measures that the experimenters have chosen to include initially (Norcross & Lambert, 2011). About thirty per cent of the variation can be predicted from characteristics of the client, twelve per cent from the quality of the therapy relationship, eight per cent from the method of therapy (e.g., CBT versus psychodynamic therapy), and seven per cent from variation between therapists (presumably due to their personal style or level of competence).

These three general conclusions from psychotherapy evaluation have been extremely influential in pushing the field in certain directions. Primarily, it has led therapists to focus on the therapy relationship or on what a client brings to therapy, given that these seem to be the chief sources of variation in therapy outcome. There is less emphasis on improving techniques because the results appear to show that they make only a small contribution to success.

I am not convinced that these conclusions from evaluation research really support the inferences that have been drawn from them. After questioning the idea of a science of psychotherapy, I will examine the reasons that are given for focusing on the client and on the therapy relationship.

A science of psychotherapy?

The scientific project of analysing "what works" in therapy sits uneasily with my suggestion that therapy has much in common with friendship. Let us suppose that scientific research into friendship were able to pinpoint exactly how to make friends and keep them, would we immediately attempt to apply it? There is a feeling that the science might be missing out something of importance. Friendship lacks the obvious pay-offs that could tell us that we had succeeded. And if a friend detects guile, it might negate any attempt to apply a technique to befriend them. In order to pursue a friendship, it is necessary to abide by certain norms that embody virtues and moral values, and the latter are not techniques.

For instance, in exchanging gifts, it should not be obvious that one gift is offered in return for another. The gift represents a sentiment, not an instrumental gesture. I do not mean to suggest that gift exchange cannot be studied scientifically, nor would it surprise me if it could be shown to comply with certain lawful rules. For instance, people commonly detect and criticise meanness and over-generosity in gift-giving, as if, at some lower level of awareness, instrumental calculations are being made.

The point is not that science cannot be applied to human behaviour but that its application as a guide to social living is by no means equivalent to the situation with other technical applications. People often suppress or discount knowledge for the sake of sustaining the social norms that govern social behaviour (Warner, 1986). For instance, even intimate partners of many years standing may suppress a secret that there is "no need" to divulge. This raises the interesting paradox of a therapist possibly having to suppress a client's awareness of the explicit employment of scientific knowledge in order to successfully apply it.

I do not mean to suggest that therapists are not justified in intending to produce change, and most clients accept that this is what they want. It is just that there are normative controls on how skills and knowledge can be employed in human relationships. How, for instance, should we compare a science of psychotherapy with a science of effective salesmanship? Should therapy limit itself to being the helpful art of facilitating a client's ability to solve his own problems or can it justify itself by drawing upon the psychological and social sciences to produce change in a deliberate and planned manner? In my view, the latter would be justified when a client is aware that a technique is being employed for a specific purpose to which he has consented. This is essentially the situation when a patient agrees to undergo a surgical operation. However, the avowed aim of acting transparently towards a client can be difficult to put into practice when the application of a therapy technique consists of very subtle interventions in the form of remarks, observations, interpretations, and even jokes. Although I do not see any obvious solution to the problem of transparency, I am not convinced that the option of strictly adhering to "scientifically validated therapies" would provide any guarantee that a technique was being employed ethically.

In an account of a proposed scientific analysis of therapy, Norcross and Lambert (2014) highlight the issue I have just raised. The essence of what they refer to as relationship science is as follows: (i) define the basic components of therapy, (ii) measure them, (iii) examine their relationship to each other and to the success of therapy, and (iv) conduct experiments to test hypotheses about how the components are causally related, in which some components are controlled. The purpose of "control" in an experiment is to hold one element constant while another is systematically varied. As Norcross and Wampold (2011) admit, this is extremely difficult to do with a phenomenon as complex as psychotherapy. In fact, to experiment in this way could be unethical. As if to underline the difficulties, these authors remind the reader that "psychotherapy is at root a human relationship" (ibid., p. 101).

The strategy of decomposing a phenomenon into its basic components and testing how they interact has a proven track record in many areas of science. However, it is not obviously suited to a personal relationship that combines all of the elements in a flowing interaction. There are critical moment-to-moment events during a session as well as differing types of interactions at various stages of therapy. A pie-chart analysis that apportions percentages to the importance of various components only makes sense if each aspect of therapy can be imagined separately and can operate independently, which of course they do not. As a practice embedded in society, all of the so-called components work together. With statistical techniques, it is possible to disassociate them into "main effects", but in fact we know that these effects interact in complex ways. The pie-chart strategy of examining which components predict a successful outcome could be compared to a recipe for making a cake (take 40% flour, 20% butter, 5% sugar, and a dose of raising agent). However, the perfect cake is a product of a fortuitous combination of ingredients and baking conditions. For example, the amount of raising agent and a certain oven temperature could be the catalyst to make a perfect cake of a certain kind but would not be optimal for all types of cake.

By way of illustration, consider the conclusion that there is insufficient evidence to show that "genuineness" (that is, congruence between the participants in what they are communicating) is a necessary element in psychotherapy (Norcross & Wampold, 2011). This only makes sense if therapy is viewed as a set of independent components, not all of which are necessary. Of course, on occasions, genuineness is not demanded; we may be impressed by a magician's tricks even though we know that the effect is due to fakery and we have paid through the nose for the entry ticket. However, I think that most people, on ethical grounds, would regard genuineness as part of the definition of a good therapy relationship and not an optional extra. If we follow the kind of scientific reasoning advocated here, the optimum therapy would appear to be a proven form of "customer care".

We should also question the implications of a science of therapy for training. Is it feasible to suppose that the caring aspects of therapy could be taught on the basis of scientific principles? Norcross & Lambert state that training programmes should be encouraged "to provide competency-based training in the demonstrably and probably effective elements of the therapy relationship" (2014, p. 401). I am not sure that this aim is compatible with the way most therapists and clients view therapy. It is questionable that training could inculcate values unless these are absorbed by osmosis while learning skills. A purely instrumental interpretation of the purposes of therapy would lead one to compare it with the services of an electrician or landscape gardener. That this would miss out something of importance is suggested by the existence of very strict professional codes of conduct. In sum, clients judge therapists against many of the norms that apply to friendship, and professional organisations seem to acknowledge this. Competence is obviously important but this may not be enough if other qualities are lacking. Norcross and Wampold (2011, p. 100) recognise this when they stress the need for "a nurturing and responsive human relationship".

I have arrived at the conclusion that the practice of psychotherapy straddles, rather uncomfortably, the twin aims of a genuine concern for another person and an instrumental desire to achieve results. A therapist uses herself as the instrument, and so the motive is not wholly dissimilar to that of a salesperson who is rewarded by a sale. At the same time, therapy is carefully regulated to ensure that it is ethical (see Chapter Eleven). I will now critique three of the inferences that have been drawn from the results of therapy evaluations.

It's got nothing to do with the therapy method

As already noted, RCTs rarely show one method of therapy to be superior to another in terms of a successful outcome. Prior to the current adoption of psychiatric criteria for effectiveness, therapists from different schools would have used a variety of measures to assess success. Consider, for the sake of illustration, a medical analogy in the form of a client with a skin complaint. A behaviour therapist would have given an ointment, a humanistic therapist would have explored empathically the significance of the complaint in the context of the client's quest to self-actualise, and the psychoanalyst would have examined the client's childhood attachments because this was assumed to be the cause of all skin complaints. In the evaluation game that is now being played out, the behaviour therapist has been the apparent winner because a reduction in the observable problem is usually seen as the best criterion for effectiveness. However, equally sharing the winnings is the psychiatric profession, which has redefined the nature of the empirical evidence to mean the presence or absence of disorders. Looking on with some relief are the health providers, health policymakers, and pharmaceutical companies who are thankful that there is no need for a wider examination of the causes of skin complaints (let us suppose them to be air pollution, work stress, side-effects of medication, diet, etc.).

The evaluation game has a great deal to do with competition between therapy brands. The intention of published articles is often "my therapy is as good as yours" or "yours is not as good as it is cracked up to be". The conclusion that all types of therapy are equally "effective" can be questioned on a number of counts. First, the concept of treatment is usually taken to mean the methods of a school or brand of therapy or some other complex combination of interventions. It is not, therefore, a concept that can be defined precisely. The proposition that techniques or methods play no part at all in contributing to the success of therapy is hardly worthy of consideration. In the dialogue between a therapist and client, knowledge and skills are constantly in play, just as they are in any joint problem-solving situation in everyday life. By a technique, I mean something that can be given concrete significance involving knowledge and skill. This definition of technique could, of course, be discounted if what I am referring to is redefined as something interpersonal and therefore subsumed under the therapy relationship. This is a tactical ploy rather than being founded on sound reasoning.

The conclusion that all methods are equally effective is only convincing when it is known how improvement has been produced. One possibility is that each therapy leads directly to changes in a complaint through its presumed causal pathways. In other words, topical ointments, reflection on life, and adverse childhood events all contribute to the mechanism of change in roughly equal amounts in the fictional medical illustration introduced earlier. This is a safe conclusion if a problem has multicausal origins and can be tackled from different directions. A second possibility is that improvement is due to factors that are common to all therapy methods. For instance, whatever the method or its underlying rationale, a client benefits by expecting to be "cured" and feels supported by a relationship with a kindly therapist. These common effects have been called non-specific because it is assumed that the administration of any technique (re-conceptualised here as a healing ritual) has a re-moralising effect (Frank, 1973). A third possibility (the most likely one, in fact) is that there is a combination of specific and non-specific causal effects in unknown combinations. If so, the null difference verdict cannot be attributed only to "common factors".

Nevertheless, most authors who agree with the Dodo bird verdict downplay the role of specific techniques. For instance, Duncan states that "because all approaches appear equal in effectiveness, there must be pantheoretical factors in operation that overshadow any perceived or presumed differences among approaches" (2002, p. 34).

Support for the Dodo bird argument could also be sought in the strong evidence that clients who do not receive therapy spontaneously improve. However, the fact that improvement appears to be spontaneous has no bearing on the manner of its explanation (i.e., non-specifically through favourable circumstances or specifically through a client's problem solving efforts). The evidence for spontaneous improvement comes from studies that have examined the outcome for clients who have been assigned to no-treatment comparison groups. It shows that, on average, thirty to forty per cent of clients resolve their own problem (an effect that is also called, in medical terms, the spontaneous remission of symptoms) (Lambert, 1976, 2013). This is clearly a very large percentage. It has also been shown that around seventeen to forty per cent of clients in therapy respond very early on, earlier than any gains would have been predicted from theory or from the application of a specific technique (Lambert, 2013). Again, this could be taken to mean that clients improve for non-specific reasons but there are no grounds for this assumption. According to Lambert, something (perhaps of a specific nature) happens to the client:

> The fact that these reported large and lasting benefits occur so early in a wide variety of treatments does suggest that the mechanisms of recovery often involve some kind of dramatic self-reorganization, which are highly dependent on client characteristics. (Ibid., p. 44)

David Orlinsky endorses the idea that therapy facilitates a process already taking place in a client. He believes it is conceivable that the finding of equivalent effectiveness for diverse forms of therapy is simply due to the fact that a high proportion of clients are psychologically minded and open to change (Orlinsky, 2009, p. 330). This explains, he argues, why well-disposed, high functioning persons can benefit from almost any sort of therapeutic intervention. However, this should not be taken to imply that common factors can be explained as non-specific effects. It is highly likely that change is due to specific kinds of decision-making or the specific employment of skills or knowledge. It is not due to "the spontaneous improvement of symptoms", a fairly meaningless phrase. The effect is only common or non-specific in the sense that therapists who belong to different schools are able to facilitate it.

Turning now to examples of the "horse race contest", Jonathan Shedler (2010) is keen to demonstrate that contemporary psychodynamic methods are as good as, if not better than, other methods. Citing evidence that uses terms reflecting the prevailing medical orthodoxy, he writes:

> The studies compared patients with a range of common mental disorders who received short term (!40 hours) psychodynamic therapy with controls (wait list, minimal treatment, or "treatment as usual") and yielded an overall effect size of 0.97 for general symptom improvement. (Ibid., p. 101)

Shedler later retracts the trust he places in medical terminology and suggests that, "Psychological health is not merely the absence of symptoms; it is the positive presence of inner capacities and resources that allow people to live life with a greater sense of freedom and possibility ... Possibly, the Dodo bird verdict reflects a failure of researchers, psychodynamic and nonpsychodynamic alike, to adequately assess the range of phenomena that can change in psychotherapy" (ibid., p. 105). In accordance with this assumption, Shedler has helped to develop an outcome scale that abandons a medical conception of mental health and substitutes a variety non-medical criteria (Shedler & Westen, 2007).

Shedler therefore "plays the game" while attempting to change its rules. He admits that we do not know what brings about change in therapy, although he cannot resist citing evidence showing that psychodynamic-type interventions seem to be the component predicting benefit in CBT, a competitor brand. Nevertheless, the situation is more or less as he states it: "What takes place in the clinical consulting room reflects the qualities and style of the individual therapist, the individual patient, and the unique patterns of interaction that develop between them" (Shedler, 2010, p. 103).

Another publication that joins in the branding exercise sets out to examine "the conjecture that one form of treatment, namely cognitive behavioral therapy (CBT), is superior to all other treatment" (Baardseth et al., 2013). The authors selected anxiety disorders, a tough test because over the past fifty years CBT has acquired its credibility through developing techniques to reduce fear and anxiety. The authors selected RCTs that compared CBT with a different *bona fide* form of therapy. Seventy-nine studies were whittled down to thirteen that had the required credentials. An interesting feature of this article is that the authors, with a somewhat surprised air, acknowledge that what they are doing is poor science:

> The ambiguity of the taxon CBT raises interesting and important issues. When talking about the essential nature of CBT, shouldn't the field be focused on those aspects of CBT that produce change? As presently conceptualized and studied, it is difficult to say what is therapeutic about CBT (or any treatment, for that matter). It seems to us that comparative trials are not advancing our knowledge. (Ibid., p. 403)

Despite these cautions, they use a sample of non-scientists (CBT practitioners) to select those RCTs that employed "real CBT" and concluded that *bona fide* CBT is no more effective than other *bona fide* therapies in terms of disorder-specific and non-disorder specific symptom measures. What are we to make of this conclusion? I imagine that nearly all CBT practitioners will simply ignore it.

It's all to do with the client

The pie-chart evidence cited earlier claims that around thirty per cent of the variation in therapy outcomes can be attributed to characteristics of the client. In my view, this is probably an underestimate given that most people sort out problems on their own without seeking therapy. The effectiveness of self-help therapy also points in this direction (see Chapter Nine). Perhaps the most important client characteristic is whether he is prepared to make a change (Prochaska & DiClemente, 1992).

There are a number of steps in this process. Initially, a person may not make a connection between a problem in his life and how he is contributing to it; later, having realised this, he may not be sure that making a change is worth the time and effort. Finally, he may resolve to pursue a plan and become fully committed to it. Of course, many clients seek therapy *before* they have actually convinced themselves about the desirability of change. Of those who are convinced, many will have begun the process of change before they ever get to see a therapist.

Client characteristics that may be of some importance in ensuring success are persistence, openness, and optimism. A client also arrives in therapy with different resources, skills, and sources of support. It will make a difference whether a client inhabits a benign environment or a hostile one that includes prejudice and misunderstanding.

In light of a recognition that clients are the chief agents of change (and not the passive recipients of "treatment") and the fact that client characteristics predict outcome, a new brand of therapy has arisen that aims to maximise a client's contribution to therapy (Sparks, Duncan & Miller, 2008). In a sense, the client is now seen as the expert. The therapist is a partner who is always attentive to a client's goals and proposed solutions to a problem. The therapist looks to the client's strengths and builds on them. The kind of relationship a therapist adopts is whatever the client perceives as most helpful. Therapists check on progress session by session with brief questionnaires to make sure that what they are offering is on target.

Viewed from the perspective of friendship, a therapist takes on the role of a supportive companion who trusts that the client knows best and wants to live a better life. This is fine as far as it goes but advice such as, "Just do what you think is best," or, "I'll support you whatever you choose," is not the kind of response that is necessarily required or expected. It might even be perceived as irritating. It lacks the cut and thrust of an active dialogue and assumes that the client does not wish to be challenged. This strategy would clearly fail if the client were to announce that she wanted to kill herself.

An exclusive emphasis on the client therefore denies the part played by a therapist's expertise and methods. If therapy had nothing to offer of a technical nature, it is difficult to explain how a generation of people diagnosed with "agoraphobia" or "compulsive rituals" sixty years ago failed to benefit from the common factors of credible therapies available at that time. I doubt that therapy of the kind proposed by

Sparks et al. (2008) would have helped them. Their recommendations are good ones but, in my view, not sufficient.

It's all about the relationship

After characteristics of the client, it is the quality of the therapy relationship that best predicts a successful therapy outcome. This evidence is correlational, and a correlation does not imply causation. There could be many reasons why a good therapy relationship is associated with a successful outcome. In research that has found a positive correlation, the quality of the relationship has been measured by scales that are completed by client or therapist, and sometimes by both parties or by an independent observer who reads transcripts or listens to session recordings. The scales are designed to capture three aspects of the relationship; first, the extent to which client and therapist are able to collaborate, second, whether they like each other, and third, whether they are able to agree on what therapy is aiming for and what tasks have to be undertaken to meet those aims (Martin, Garske & Davis, 2000).

The significance that has been attached to the quality of the relationship between therapist and client appears, at first glance, to support the idea that therapy and friendship have much in common. However, I have stressed the virtues and norms of friendship rather than any notion that the relationship is the cause of a good outcome. Friends, like therapists, can be badly chosen, and in some cases a close friend would be the last person one would want to go to for advice. However, we expect friends to be trustworthy and "true to themselves", and to engage with us voluntarily rather than under any compulsion. Similar assumptions operate in therapy. These are some of the preconditions for therapy, rather than a guarantee of a productive relationship.

The first point to make about measures of the quality of the therapy relationship (sometimes called the alliance or therapeutic bond) is that they contain a mixed bag of constituents. As Krause, Altimir, and Horvath point out when they review research in the area:

> The alliance is thought to be a factor in all helping relations but it is not an integral part of a formal theory or logical chain of ideas linked together to account for how psychological growth can occur. (2011, p. 268)

The consensus amongst expert therapists seems to be that there are complex interactions between features of the relationship, a client's characteristics and preferences, and therapy techniques (Geller, 2005; Goldfried & Davila, 2005; Hill, 2005). It is therefore artificial to separate out the relationship from other factors. It has become almost a slogan to announce, "It's the relationship, stupid." Samuels (2014) believes that this claim is something worse than a cliché and that actual harm might be being done.

One explanation for the correlation between the quality of the therapy relationship and an ultimately successful outcome is the obvious one that if clients perceive their therapist as competent, caring, and likable, they are more likely to engage seriously with the process of change. This is, however, a two-way process. Well-motivated clients may be more liked by their therapist and given greater encouragement. This may in turn may increase a client's inclination to attend diligently and participate in all therapy tasks (Holdsworth, Bowen, Brown & Howat, 2014).

The significance that attaches to the relationship originated with early psychoanalytic theory. As we saw in Chapter Four, it was important to analyse the feelings that were experienced by client and therapist within a session, at both conscious and unconscious levels of awareness (the transference and countertransference). The significance of the therapy relationship is also evident in Carl Rogers' focus on genuineness, empathy, and unconditional positive regard, which has been hugely influential (Feller & Cottone, 2003).

Another aspect of the relationship follows naturally from the fact that therapy is a service with a purpose. The working alliance can be defined as everything that promotes a business-like collaboration, that is, coming to an agreement about what therapy is for (its goals) and a commitment to work towards them in an agreed way.

In the psychoanalytic tradition, the relationship can be considered from the point of view of "distorted" and "undistorted" perceptions of what each partner is feeling or thinking (Gelso & Carter, 1994, Gelso, 2011). This division of communication into two types permits these authors to speak of the "real relationship" that refers to accurate perceptions of the feelings and personal qualities of the other person. In their opinion, therapist and client might genuinely like or dislike each other, independently of transference responses that distort their relationship. Although a distinction between distorted and undistorted perceptions seems sound, it has to be admitted that in everyday (supposedly undistorted) interactions, it is common to misjudge people based on preconceived notions and prejudices. In fact, Greenberg (1994) questions the basis of Gelso and Carters' distinction.

Whether based on real or unreal perceptions, an intuited sense that a therapy relationship feels right or wrong is probably a strong determinant of whether a client sticks with it. Around twenty per cent of clients leave therapy before it has got underway, and this suggests that the process of finding a good match is not an easy one (Swift & Greenberg, 2012). Research shows that clients rate the alliance more consistently across sessions than do therapists or observers. This suggests that a client's intuited sense of a right match is strongly felt and enduring. In very long-term forms of therapy, however, there is a good chance that the quality of the relationship will change. This is especially so in psychodynamic therapies where an analysis of the nature of the relationship is seen as the mechanism of change.

In the next chapter I will examine ways in which a therapy relationship is vulnerable to going badly wrong or, worse, can lead to abuse.

CHAPTER SEVEN

Therapy: Cracks in the foundations

This chapter brings together a variety of themes that relate to potential weaknesses in therapy as a service and as an occupation.

Power imbalance

For Jefffrey Masson (1988) psychotherapy is so hopelessly flawed that he feels the practice should be abolished. Whether or not clients appreciate its benefits, Masson believes that there is an inherent imbalance of power between the one who is an "expert" and the one in trouble. He supplies ample and convincing evidence that therapists can be prejudiced, exploitative, and downright harmful. He thinks the practice is a sham because a therapist is paid for the service and profits from another's misery. He argues that a client doesn't really get to know the therapist, who may act very differently outside the artificial setting of an office. In other words, the warmth and interest are just an act. If we accept Masson's criticisms, therapy cannot be compared with a friendship in which, ideally, there is genuineness and an absence of power and hierarchy.

The word power conjures up the picture of one person controlling another for selfish ends. One example would be to prolong therapy for an unnecessarily long period of time in order to profit financially. If we recast power in a neutral sense to mean "determining what happens", then a therapist must exert power, otherwise therapy would meander along without any purpose at all. The client, as a willing collaborator, is also able to determine what happens by controlling the release of personal information and by initiating changes in her life. Both participants exert power, and this can be a productive and balanced relationship. In a piece of research that sampled clients' opinions about the therapy they had received, clients preferred therapists who used positive strategies rather than coercive ones but they also had regard for their therapist as an expert, a quality they associated with the success of their therapy (McCarthy & Frieze, 1999).

Typically, therapists want clients to take control of their own destiny, and so they employ their power in order to surrender it. Of course, it cannot be assumed that clients are strongly inclined to take control in a way that leads to their ultimate objective. Their efforts to do so with a therapist may divert attention onto irrelevancies. Rather than "take the bull by the horns", clients might prevaricate by focusing on impediments to action. Therapists may be rendered powerless for these reasons or come to the conclusion that clients do not really want what they professes to want (or are not yet ready to make a change). To influence another is a very delicate business because most people prefer that any initiative comes from themselves alone. Consequently, a therapist's influence may have to be disguised or indirect. In many cases, therapists may not really know in what way they have been helpful, even when the outcome has been successful. For instance, a client may have picked up on something a therapist has said in passing as it were.

In a study designed to understand what is meant by the exercise of power in counselling sessions, Terence Tracey (1991) used various systems of coding to pick out behaviour that could be interpreted as the exercise of power. One form was called "domineeringness", which was the tendency of either party to instruct or direct. Given that direct attempts to control can be ignored, another relevant measure was dominance, which took account of the effect of an attempt to domineer. Another measure disregarded the way behaviour could be classified and simply coded whether one response was predictably followed by another, and therefore, in a sense, controlled it. For instance, a client's expression of helplessness might be regularly followed by a therapist's attempt to reassure and help. If this pattern takes up most of a session, a client could be said to be holding the power within it.

It is of some interest that in this study clients' perceptions of the control exerted by therapists bore no relationship to the behavioural measures of control just outlined. This suggests that the whole process of mutual influence is rather opaque. Perhaps the researcher's method was at fault, and an analysis of what the participants intended by their words and actions would have been more informative. One of Tracey's interesting findings was that the amount of control exerted by the client was positively related to the amount exerted by the therapist. This makes sense; a productive use of power is when each participant exerts control over the other in a *quid pro quo*.

This conclusion fits in well with Nick Totton's (2006) observations on power in psychotherapy. For him, therapy has to respect truth. This means cultivating awareness of values and beliefs and acknowledging important differences of position between therapist and client. A rapprochement is negotiated in so far as this is necessary when the nature of a problem calls for it. In some cases, a rapprochement may be hard to achieve. For instance, when a client perceives a therapist as a repository of wisdom and expertise, a therapist may be tempted to fall into the trap of supplying it. Another problem commonly arises when a client has a history of being subjugated by powerful caregivers against whom deferment was the only safe response. In this case, a therapist may be perceived as an adversary to battle with or as an authority figure to submit to. Power and control are central to the client's difficulties.

Therapists normally attempt to encourage a client's autonomy and self-assertion. This may involve supporting a client against friends, relations, employers, or societal agencies that are maintaining her state of powerlessness. A subjugated person who already lacks the strength for this undertaking may quite reasonably lean on the advice and support of a therapist who is advocating it. In other words, therapists necessarily exercise power and this is not always a bad influence.

If a therapy relationship is necessarily one of unequal power, in which the friendship it appears to offer is somehow a fake replica, one would expect a number of complaints from clients that they have been "used". When others claim falsely to be friends for their personal advantage, they are heavily censored when found out. It is certainly true that clients (and indeed their therapists) can feel let down at times, but complaints still seem to be rather rare (see Chapter Eleven). The evidence is that despite criticism and documented abuses, counselling and psychotherapy have become increasingly popular over recent years. Clients probably accept that a therapist is not a friend in the usual sense of the word and realise that there can be no guarantee that a problem will be resolved.

Sex

Therapy is not intended to develop into a sexual relationship but according to surveys this is not infrequently one of its consequences (Garrett, 1994). A sexual relationship with a client during therapy, if discovered, normally results in a therapist being prohibited from practising by the professional body that licenses them. The situation is less clear after therapy ends. Opinions differ as to whether the prohibition against a sexual relationship should be permanent or only continue for a certain length of time afterwards.

To deny that sexual attraction can be a component of a therapy relationship would make the latter into a rather abnormal, closeted activity, hedged around with artificial prohibitions. However, a sexual attraction is not something that has to represent a problem, any more than in daily life, a person does not go around signalling an attraction for anyone found attractive. Sometimes, sexual feelings generated in therapy can be strong, and one party, or both, may wish to act upon them. The intimacy of the relationship raises the probability of this happening, and it is also encouraged by a style of therapy that deliberately focuses on the feelings that exist between client and therapist. However, sexual feelings cannot always be attributed to transference or countertransference that have their origin in projections and idealisations carried over from a client's (or therapist's) earlier relationships. Therefore, the feelings do not necessarily represent an unreal "distortion". Nevertheless, it seems likely that relationships started on the basis of transference would end badly.

The situation in which loving and sexual feelings threaten to scupper therapy is sensitively discussed by Gelso, Rojas, and Marmarosh (2013). The authors note that this is not a situation that can be brushed aside and left unacknowledged. They illustrate the problem with two clients who expressed sexual feelings, and in one case the feelings were reciprocated. A client's expression of sexual longing can have a variety of interpretations. It could be a way of asking for acceptance, a rejection of being placed in the client role, a way of feeling special, a test of power, a fear of relating in an intimate non-sexual way, or an expression of dependency.

In the example they provide of mutual sexual attraction, these feelings seemed to have been based partly (for the therapist) on the client's physical attractiveness, a feeling of loneliness, and a shared theme in personal histories (death of a family member through illness). Gelso and colleagues suggest that a therapist's caring for a client may contain "a healthy sexual element", but not one that should be developed or encouraged given the cautions already stated.

Therapists who have problems themselves

Clients are sometimes puzzled by a therapist's willingness to choose an occupation that involves listening to other people's problems. One suspicion is that therapists are motivated by a desire to sort out problems of their own or to obtain gratification by listening to the intimacies of another's life.

There has been rather little interest in studying the kind of person who is attracted to train in psychotherapy. In a review of the literature, Michael Sussman (2007, p. 2) points out that it has been a neglected area. Sussman tends to focus on all the reprehensible and pathological motives for taking on the role. He believes that doing therapy requires "feminine character traits", and that males who are attracted to it may not have completely resolved their childhood oedipal conflicts (ibid., p.178). I have a sense that his opinions have been rather too heavily influenced by his psychoanalytic training.

In one survey, nearly half of therapists admitted that they were attracted to the job because they wanted to explore and resolve their own personal problems (Orlinsky & Ronnestad, 2005). This does not necessarily imply that they continued to experience these problems or that their performance as therapists had suffered as a result. In fact, quite the reverse was suggested in a study of female therapists by Elliott and Guy (1993). They compared a large sample of mental health professionals with an even larger sample of women who had entered unrelated professions. The former group had suffered higher rates of physical abuse and sexual molestation in childhood, an alcoholic or mentally ill parent, or death of a parent. They were also more likely to have received psychotherapy themselves. As adults, the two groups of women reported equivalent (low) rates of substance abuse or hospitalisation for a mental illness. Rather surprisingly, the women working in professions that were *not* in the mental health field reported higher levels of anxiety, depressed mood, feelings of dissociation, disturbed sleep, and were more likely to have interpersonal difficulties. It is possible that the mental health professionals were more willing to examine and deal with any problems they experienced as adults. They may have learned to do this as children by taking on a "caretaker role" with parents. This interpretation finds echoes in some of the reasons that therapists give for taking up their profession (Spurling & Dryden, 1989).

Therapist stress and burn-out

Therapy is not an easy job, and a group of experienced therapists were motivated to get together to share and describe their difficulties (Davis et al., 1987). Three of the difficulties they came up with can be understood as a consequence of a tendency to be self-critical. The therapists asked themselves: Could I have done things differently or better? Have I caused harm? How can I get around this problem that I don't understand very well? Sometimes they felt stuck in their attempt to work towards therapy objectives, which in some cases appeared to be the result of a client actively thwarting their efforts. Therapists also blamed themselves when they felt that their own personal issues (feelings, beliefs, or values that were unrelated to therapy) were interfering.

One category of difficulties concerned a threatening or hostile client. Another was feeling at a loss in developing rapport, being unable to like a client, or just failing to find a common language. The therapists also described ethical dilemmas. One was feeling powerless to change a painful reality affecting a client (e.g., a terminal illness). Occasionally, they could not decide which course of action was ethically preferable, for example, where an obligation to a client was in conflict with an obligation to others or in conflict with a professional code of conduct.

Deutsch (1984), in a questionnaire survey of stress experienced by psychotherapists, listed the following causes in order of importance: 1. Clients' suicidal statements, 2. Inability to help an acutely distressed client, 3. Clients' expression of anger towards the therapist, 4. Clients' lack of progress. The threat of suicide happened in eleven per cent of contact hours or about twice a week on average. Deutsch also asked therapists about their beliefs about practising therapy. The replies suggested that therapists had very high standards of performance for themselves. A high level of stress was probably related to a failure to live up to their own expectations.

It should come as no surprise that there has been considerable interest in the possibility of therapists suffering "burnout", a concept that was invented around fifty years ago by a psychoanalyst working in a free clinic in New York (Friberg, 2009). Given that the clinic offered help to marginalised and needy persons, it is easy to imagine that the demands placed on therapists working there could never be satisfied. In a later clarification of the concept, "burnout" was described as consisting of overwhelming exhaustion, feelings of cynicism, detachment from the job, dehumanisation of clients, and a sense of professional ineffectiveness (Maslach, Schaufeli & Leiter, 2001). The concept has been applied to a variety of occupations that provide a personal service, such as nursing or the police force.

Burnout is related to another concept called emotion work (Hochschild, 1983). For Arlie Hochschild, emotion work means being required to display the emotions that befit the service, which in many industries is commonly pleasantness in the face of a customer's hostility or indifference. The effort involved in meeting this demand is presumably greatest when the employee is actually experiencing a quite different frame of mind, such as irritation or sadness. Emotion work is therefore rather like a right-handed person trying to write with his left hand. Hochschild regards it as a form of human exploitation, leading to alienation and effects on health. Emotion work requires employees to be sensitive to different kinds of emotion in their dealings with the public (Zapf, Vogt, Seifert, Mertini & Isic, 1999). Whether this is experienced as hard work depends on how much control workers have in handling a situation, and how much their real feelings are at variance with the ones they are expected to display.

Psychotherapy is unquestionably emotion work because it would be a very poor therapist who did not convey the feeling that it was possible for a client to change, even though privately he might have reservations or feel downright pessimistic. However, in therapy, and perhaps more so than in any other personal service, there are emotional rewards as well as emotional costs. Furthermore, a therapist ought to be in a position to exert considerable control over how he responds to an emotionally distressed client. There are no prescribed rules or patter, as in a call centre.

The concept of emotion work is more germane to the employment of therapy techniques whose strategic purpose, if not unknown to a client, is at least partially concealed. Analogous behaviours in daily life would be "buttering up", "taking liberties", or "mocking", when the recipient is only partially unaware of how he is being treated. In therapy, the intention is, of course, to benefit a client, not to undermine him. Any sign of a client resisting change, or any demand he makes that comes across to a therapist as unreasonable, is usually taken to be an expression of his problem, not something that a therapist should take personally. Jacqueline Persons (2008, p. 170) gives an example of being irritated by a client who did not thank her for accommodating his request for an inconvenient appointment time or apologise when he later cancelled it. His behaviour seemed to be another example of the kind of problem he was having with his work colleagues. Rather than acting in line with her true feelings (e.g., postponing a call back, imposing an appointment time, or being a bit cool) she returned his call, using a warm, pleasant tone that would facilitate a productive discussion of the rescheduling topic, which also related it to his problems at work. This strategy was probably of benefit to him but involved emotion work on the part of Persons.

The leverage a therapist can exert when he acts strategically in his personal interactions with a client depends on having first established a good relationship. In the words of Marsha Linehan, "the therapist first develops a strong positive relationship and then uses it to 'blackmail' the patient into making targeted, but excruciatingly difficult, changes in her behavior" (1993, p. 296).

According to Carl Rogers, and for many of his followers, it is important for a therapist to be genuine in what he says and feels. The more he achieves this, the less dissonant will be his handling of, say, a client's anger or despair. Of course, in his personal life, a therapist might deal with a comparable situation in a very different way. This should not be taken to imply a lack of genuineness if a therapist knows what he is doing and has a client's interest at heart. It should be possible for a therapist to act skillfully when responding to a client's negative emotions without sacrificing his own genuineness. In any case, a problem can always be discussed or role-played with a client as a "let's pretend" situation. This brackets off the question of genuineness when therapist and client display "as if" emotions when acting them out. Both participants can learn a great deal about why a problem has occurred or how it could be handled differently. Assertiveness training relies heavily on this kind role-playing.

Work as a therapist contains a number of stressful aspects. Regardless of the type of work, it would be normal to expect exhaustion and cynicism when the level of demand is unreasonably high. A case can be made for distinguishing burnout from stress, the former referring to a loss of the sense that work is meaningful, useful, or important (Pines & Keinan, 2005). Burnout might be expected in careers that call for idealistic goals, especially when a person enters them with high expectations.

There are positive compensations as well. Linley and Joseph (2007) assessed a sense of personal growth and the value therapists attached to life as a result of their work. Those with the longest careers reported more negative changes and compassion fatigue but a high current workload was associated with positive effects. Therapists who showed least burnout were those who perceived the world as comprehensible, manageable, and meaningful, and it helped if they were receiving (or had received) personal therapy. A sense of personal growth through working as a therapist was associated with forming strong personal attachments with clients, with being a woman, with having a personal history of trauma, and with receiving formal supervision for therapy work.

Therapists are vulnerable to stress because they often have to listen to harrowing accounts of abuse, trauma, or torture. These are first-hand intimate accounts rather than second-hand reports in other media. It has been found that working with trauma can produce secondary traumatisation of a therapist (Elwood, Mott, Lohr & Galovski, 2011). It is not uncommon to work with clients who intentionally self-harm by cutting into their skin or by burning themselves. These are not usually lethal attempts to end their own life but more likely to be a way of coping with unbearable emotional feelings. Therapists have used words such as "shocking", "heartbreaking" and "absolute terror" to describe their own reactions to problems of this kind (Fleet & Mintz, 2013). They may also feel anger and frustration, in some cases directed towards medical professionals who deal with their client in a punitive manner.

Another potential source of stress is the requirement to maintain an upbeat attitude. A therapist cannot easily plead to be excused from work for weeks at a time when she is severely stressed herself by, say, a bereavement or other unforeseen circumstance. Another important source of stress comes from a sense of responsibility for another's wellbeing. Therapy depends on building up a relationship of trust that carries with it a client's expectation of support and help. Consequently, therapists may feel that they have let a client down when they are unable to resolve a problem. Moreover, they often work independently, in isolation, without sufficient personal or structural support. Their work is closely regulated to ensure that they have not been negligent or departed from codes of conduct in even minor ways. A false accusation from a client, even when successfully defended, could result in a therapist having her whole career and source of income prematurely extinguished.

There are research reports showing that up to ten per cent of therapists continue working despite feeling too distressed to be really effective. In a study of therapists and their clients, Zeeck, Orlinsky, Hermann, Joos, Wirsching, Weidmann, and Hartmann (2012) found that twenty-seven per cent of therapists were practising in a "disengaged" manner, and ten per cent in a distressed mode. Therapists varied in the average number of their positive and negative experiences with clients but there was just as much variability within each therapist. In other words, some clients presented them with difficulties and others did not.

Zeeck and colleagues observed a difference between therapists' and clients' perceptions. For therapists, negative experiences (especially a sense of discouragement between sessions) were strongly related to the emotional bond they had established with a client, but this was not true for clients. Therapists who rated their own personality as unassertive, socially inhibited, or vindictive were also more likely to experience stress within and between sessions. It should be noted that their personality scores were all within the normal range, and vindictiveness scores were actually lower, on average, than in the general population. The highest score on the personality questionnaire was on a trait labelled as being "overly accommodated/exploited". This suggests that these therapists thought they needed to be super-accommodating in order to work effectively, and that they were complicit in adopting an attitude consistent with this requirement. In this study at least, it may have laid them open to experiencing greater stress.

I can offer two examples of occupational hazards from personal experience. The first involved a man who I felt, over a number of weeks, was becoming increasingly suicidal. Discussion with work colleagues supported my analysis but I received no direct advice as to how to proceed.

At a session when my apprehension was raised further, I discussed him with a psychiatrist at the emergency clinic of the hospital at which I was working. My client attended there after my session and I expected him to be admitted. He was not admitted and he took his own life later that evening.

A second example was a twenty-year-old woman living alone in accommodation provided by social services. She was estranged from her family, having left home and been placed in care. She regularly cut herself, and had recently suffered two major traumas. The first was a near-fatal road traffic accident which resulted in bodily disfigurement, and the second, shortly after the accident, was the murder by stabbing of a friend. It was Christmas and her twenty-first birthday was coming up in January, for neither of which she had any plans. As she had failed to attend and had not responded to several communications, I asked her social worker to visit in order to check how she was, as I suspected that she was neglecting herself and feeling depressed, if not suicidal. The social worker declined, saying that she had not been "invited" by my client to visit her. Her general practitioner, with whom she had recently registered, had never met her and he told me that he knew nothing about psychiatry. The local community mental health team refused to visit her, having recently been instructed to raise their threshold for taking on new clients.

In light of my concern, I decided to send a text message offering to visit her myself, to which she agreed. This was professionally risky in view of the fact that I was a male therapist visiting a young vulnerable woman. If she had falsely accused me of molesting her in some way, this would have been taken seriously by my regulator, details of allegations would have been published before any hearing could have taken place, leading to the end of my practice and reputation. On the other hand, if she took her own life, I could suffer the same fate for not having been sufficiently proactive in preventing it. Having made the visit (which she seemed to appreciate) I remained concerned that she was depressed and neglecting herself. I therefore wrote to her social worker and GP, reminding them that they could be responsible for a suicide if no action were taken. It was then that two workers from the community mental health team were induced to pay a visit. Whereas it would have been helpful to continue my involvement, having built up a good relationship with my client, this was not possible because her therapy was funded by insurance (relating to the road traffic accident) and they did not agree to extend it. They presumably would argue that her needs were largely unrelated to the consequences of her accident. The mental health team offered further appointments but she did not attend them. (If I had offered to continue to see her without payment, this would have been liable to misinterpretation). I was contacted a year later by her solicitor as my (now) ex-client had suggested I might be someone who could verify that she had mental capacity to accept a motor insurance payout. I inferred from this that she had not seen any other mental health professional in the meantime.

Most therapists could probably produce examples similar to these two, where a therapist is the last link in a chain of help. In these circumstances a therapist is obliged to consider all of the needs of a client, which is very different from playing a contributory role (e.g., in the example above, the GP, social worker, and the motor vehicle insurer). Even when a therapist receives supervision and works in a highly structured organisation, this might not mitigate the felt level of responsibility. Any therapist tempted to take on the mantle of rescuer is likely to experience considerable stress in these circumstances. Given typical motivations for entering the profession, a therapist is set up to feel guilt or a sense of failure when a client cannot be helped.

The therapist as "special friend"

If a therapist is indeed a "special kind of friend" what does this tell us about the way therapists conduct themselves? Different friends evoke different styles of relating. Some like to be taken very seriously, others enjoy being ribbed. Some tolerate aggressive bickering, while others wilt under the palest of criticisms. Some ask for direct advice, others want only a disguised hint. If one is going to pitch in with definite advice, it is best done tactfully. A similar matching of "styles" is probably needed in therapy.

A therapist can get things wrong in a variety of ways. Marvin Goldfried (2013) reiterates the principle of starting where the client is at. This means carefully following the reasons a client supplies for acting as he does. Leading a client in a new direction is more likely to be successful when the point of departure (where the client is at) has become quite clear. Clients vary enormously in their receptivity to advice. For some, even an innocuous suggestion is an implied criticism. The safest course seems to be patience. A common cause of impatience is a client not responding to a technique as expected, when there is a temptation to carry on regardless. Another cause is therapists setting their sights too high, for instance, expecting someone who is a born introvert to become a raging extrovert. It is necessary to respect the fact that clients may have limited goals.

As is true of friends, clients and therapists adapt to each other. A good relationship is therefore one that "fits", feels comfortable, and, at the same time, does the business. The aim of therapy might be "to console, to clarify, to exemplify, to inspire, to explain, and so forth" and it should promote "collaboration, intimacy, trust, and mutual respect" (Geller, 2005, p. 468). Although Jesse Geller describes what he does as "healing", it bears a close resemblance to what we can expect from friendship: a sincere effort to be understood, receiving feedback without blame on how we are coming across, being able to talk about painful feelings, being confronted with our obstinacy about making a change, and inspiring hope.

According to Geller, an empathic understanding of a client's account of his difficulties does two things. First, it externalises them, or as Francis Bacon expressed it, discoursing with a friend "bringeth his owne Thoughts to Light, and whetteth his Wits against a Stone, which it selfe cuts not" (see Chapter Two). Second, discussion allows a therapist's thoughts, feelings, facial expressions, gestures, values, and attitudes to be internalised by the client in a new private self-dialogue. This does not mean the wholesale incorporation of a therapist's response to a problem but an ability to consider it from multiple perspectives. A client might remark: "In that situation, I remembered what you said last week about …".

I recall one woman who regularly telephoned me when she felt suicidal, seeking reassurance that she was a worthwhile person and should not take her own life. Seeing that she could not keep on doing this, she suggested that I record my words on her answering machine, so that she could be reminded of them as needed. This is an example of the way communication within a session can be made overt and can be internalised outside it. A good relationship with a therapist is not, therefore, simply a matter of mutual liking and respect. It involves really being listened to without censure and hearing back something interesting and relevant to one's concerns. It is not a purely verbal process; clients are equally attuned to a therapist's hesitation or silence after having said something that seemed to them important. On occasion, clients do not like what they hear, and such "ruptures" in the relationship, as they are usually called, need mending. If repeated and unresolved, a good relationship becomes a bad or non-existent one. A good therapist is therefore one who responds in a non-defensive manner to unflattering or critical remarks. The same could be said of a good friend (or at least of a person who wants to remain a friend).

CHAPTER EIGHT

The client's perspective

It is commonly assumed that therapy is very popular and that people are clamouring for an increase in its availability. We have a survey of a representative sample of the UK population carried out in 2007 that questions this assumption. It asked respondents whether they found it easy to talk about their feelings and whether they would see a therapist if given the chance (Anderson & Brownlie, 2011). Around half to two-thirds of the people interviewed found it easy to talk about their feelings and thought that it was important to do so. However, this was much less true for the over sixty-fives and for males of all ages. When it came to actually talking to a professional, it seems there was considerable resistance to the idea, especially in some sections of the population. Only around a third of people would feel comfortable talking to a therapist, and over forty per cent wouldn't want anyone to know about it if they did. Young males (aged 18–24) were most resistant to the idea; eighty per cent did not agree that they would feel comfortable talking to a therapist.

Over the whole sample, only sixteen per cent had ever seen a therapist, counsellor, or mental health professional. The reason given for not seeking professional help was not difficulty of access, unavailability, or lack of knowledge. It was simply that "the problem resolved itself" (31%) or they "didn't believe it would make any difference" (29%).

Around one in five persons had considered seeking it out but had not done so. Those who had had experience of therapy in the past were actually twice as likely *not* to want to seek it again (31% compared with 16% of those with no previous experience). These findings suggest that people are sceptical about therapy, and there is little to indicate that we all belong to a "therapy culture". The response rate in this survey was fifty-one per cent, and it is possible that those who didn't give their views were even more sceptical.

I conclude that people are not fighting to avail themselves of therapy, whether free at the point of delivery or obtained privately. This could be due to a number of reasons, such as lack of knowledge of what it has to offer, unsatisfactory previous experience, or a stoical attitude to life. The authors suggest that perhaps the boundary between formal and informal help should become blurred, allowing therapists to work in community settings that are less formal. However, in view of increasingly strict statutory and professional regulation of the working life of therapists, it is unlikely that they would want to take the risk of working in this way. They would then lay themselves open to technical breaches of professional boundaries or false accusations of inappropriate behaviour (see Chapter Eleven).

Finding a "good" therapist

A person who decides to seek help will want to find a good therapist. Those in this position should consider what kind of approach they would prefer and look for someone who is known to have expertise in solving the kind of problem for which they seek help. It is somewhat easier to find a good dentist because in this case the technical requirements are much clearer, and a search would be guided mainly by reputation. Age, gender, and cultural background are unlikely to be considered important. Whether a dentist was likable might matter a little more, but might not be critical. By contrast, a person choosing a therapist faces greater uncertainty. The causes of his problem may be unclear to him and so he may not know who to approach. Having decided this, he would probably want to feel comfortable with his chosen therapist, and in this respect age, gender, and cultural background might influence his choice. A recently qualified therapist might be viewed with suspicion whereas a recently qualified dentist might be preferred on the basis that she is likely to be more familiar with the latest techniques.

Therapy involves a far greater degree of collaboration than does dentistry or, indeed, most medical procedures. A therapist must be highly attentive to what a client says but any pearls of wisdom will fall by the wayside if a client is not ready to receive them. We all know how hard it is for a friend to heed your good advice; "He's going into it blindly," "She won't listen," "He's a lost cause," are typical refrains. Consequently, the first task facing a therapist is to recruit and mobilise a client's own resources for solving his problem. It would be surprising to find a client who did not believe this as well. A therapist's expertise is on conditional loan as it were.

A potential client has rather few pointers in his search for someone who is generally acknowledged to be "really good" at what they do. There are different approaches to therapy to choose from, and expertise with one type of problem does not imply expertise in others. There have been a few attempts to research the qualities of those therapists who are regarded as being particularly outstanding. Jennings and Skovholt (1999) interviewed ten individuals who were carefully selected from a larger pool through having been repeatedly nominated by their professional colleagues as exceptional. As a group they exhibited the following personal qualities: they valued learning from experience and the continual acquisition of knowledge; they welcomed the ambiguity and complexity of the human condition; they seemed to be self-aware, non-defensive, and open to feedback; they valued authenticity and honesty; they were able to relate strongly to others, which in part seemed to stem from experiences in their own family of origin; they were caring and empathic, firmly believing that clients could change. The authors concluded that these master therapists had a blend of skills but wondered if they were tapping into the qualities of individuals who would function well in any field. Perhaps they were nominated by colleagues simply because they were attractive and admirable people.

In another study, fourteen acknowledged experts in psychotherapy were questioned about the way they attempted to raise clients' awareness of the nature of their problems and to change them (Levitt & Williams, 2010). Despite adopting very different theoretical and technical approaches, these experts seemed to share common intentions. The process they described is what one would expect if therapy is understood to be a problem-solving activity. They stressed the need to develop clients' curiosity and to encourage clients to explore emotionally charged topics. Their aim was to provide a safe environment in which to encounter threat, and to assist clients in integrating and understanding their new experiences. These experts seemed to be proficient at helping their clients explore and solve problems. It seems that ineffective or harmful therapists are less able to do this; they may be uncertain, critical, distant, tense, or distracted (Ackerman & Hilsenroth, 2001).

Variation in therapists' effectiveness

There is evidence to show that therapists vary a great deal in their effectiveness (Okiishi, Lambert, Nielson & Ogles, 2003; Wampold & Brown, 2005; Lutz, Leon, Lyons, Martinowitz & Stiles, 2007). While some therapists may be highly effective with certain clients, they may leave a proportion of their clientele worse off than when they first consulted. One study investigated the results obtained with ten clients each of 696 therapists, giving a total of 6,960 clients (Kraus, Castonguay, Boswell, Nordberg & Hayes, 2011). The clients were given scales to complete before and after therapy measuring twelve different areas of "symptoms" and social functioning. The effectiveness of therapists was judged by whether or not they produced a reliable change in scores in each area. On this basis, they were divided into effective therapists, harmful therapists, and a group in between. According to averaged scores, clients treated by harmful therapists were significantly worse off than when they started therapy. It was found that a therapist who was effective with one type of problem was not necessarily effective in another. In most problem areas, the proportion of harmful therapists was less than ten per cent, but for certain problems (sexual and social functioning, substance abuse, and violence) it was as high as sixteen per cent. However, it was possible to find a substantial number of therapists who were able to work effectively with these types of problem. One lesson that potential clients should take from this study is to always choose a therapist with specialised experience. Ninety-six per cent of therapists were effective in at least one area of work.

Whether or not a therapy is counted as successful depends to some extent on whether a client, when she enters therapy, is on a trajectory of improvement, no change, or deterioration (Dimidjian & Hollon, 2010). For instance, we can ask whether a problem would have remained the same without therapy or would have resolved itself spontaneously if left alone because the client was already on an improving course.

When a client is on a downward course, therapy might not resolve a problem but could act as a prop that prevents it from getting worse. It is therefore difficult to know whether a therapeutic method is beneficial, on average, unless a comparison is made with a group of clients, selected at random from the same pool, who have not received it. It is also necessary to take account of a wide variety of possible outcomes, given that solving one problem could create new ones or exacerbate others.

It would be natural to assume that therapists who are more successful with their clients would demonstrate greater competence or skill. In research I cite below, this has not been found to be the case, and the cause of this paradox may lie in the difficulty of defining what competence and success actually mean. Researchers have typically employed checklists of psychiatric symptoms and scales of social well-being to assess the success of an outcome. Although these measures are likely to capture some of the benefits for most clients, they are very general in nature. In practice, clients and therapists usually negotiate unique goals at the beginning of therapy, making it clear what therapy is aiming to achieve. It is sometimes the case that the goals are unambiguous (such as abstinent or controlled drinking, weight gain or weight loss, or overcoming insomnia) but for many clients what they want to get out of therapy is much more difficult to classify. In humanistic and psychodynamic therapies, a successful outcome would not necessarily be equated with a specific change in behaviour or mood. Given the variety of reasons for which therapy is sought, a measure of success that applies across all clients is very difficult to construct.

It is also difficult to define competence in a general sense. The skills of the cognitive therapist and psychoanalyst are very different. There may be some personal qualities, interpersonal skills, and theoretical knowledge that all effective therapists share in common but they have not yet been agreed. It is also unreasonable to suppose that the skills required for working with different client populations would be the same. Certain problems are known to be very difficult to resolve and so, in this case, a therapist's average level of success could be quite modest.

Setting aside all these conceptual difficulties, researchers have assessed the competence exhibited by therapists in their sessions of therapy and related it to the success of the outcome. The method for assessing competence has been to recruit independent judges who rate audio or video recordings of therapy sessions. The raters may focus on the extent to which a therapist is adhering to prescribed techniques.

Naturally, adherence has a different meaning according to the type of therapy being delivered. A psychoanalyst and a cognitive therapist will work differently, but nevertheless faithfully, in the light of their own aims and methods. The results of thirty-six different studies of therapists' competence, or adherence to technique, have recently been reviewed by Webb, DeRubeis, and Barber (2010). The rather surprising conclusion of this review was that, on average, across all the studies, therapists' adherence to a method or their general competence bore no relationship whatsoever to the success they achieved. Potential clients may be somewhat alarmed by this finding. It seems to imply that whether or not the therapist they select helps them to achieve their goals is a matter of pot luck.

Webb and colleagues found slight evidence that a therapist's competence did matter when the problem was severe depression, and there is other evidence that competence is related to outcome, especially in cognitive behavioural therapy (Trepka, Rees, Shapiro, Hardy & Barkham, 2004; Westra, Constantino, Arkowitz & Dozois, 2011). However, the overall message is clear: having a competent therapist is not any guarantee of securing benefit. The best strategy seems to be to choose someone with a good track record of success in the kind of problem for which help is being sought. Of course, clients also need to be open to advice, willing to experiment, and proactive on their own behalf. If these conditions are not in place, even the most brilliant of therapists is unlikely to have much impact.

What do clients expect from therapy?

A variety of messages about therapy are relayed by the media; scepticism or debunking are frequently more common than praise. The public's understanding of what therapy has to offer is probably in a constant state of flux. About forty years ago, the expectations of people presenting themselves for the first time to public outpatient psychiatric clinics, were, in one study, as follows (Freeman & Viney, 1977). Some clients expected therapists to be empathic and personally committed to them, others expected the professional to take a more businesslike approach and be matter of fact. Clients also varied in expecting a therapist to be either confrontational or to avoid hurting their feelings. In the former case, it was thought that a therapist might help them face up to things or even be "hard on them". The authors of the study noted that there were large individual differences in the extent to which clients expected a genuine, natural, and personal approach from their therapist rather than "professional reserve". The former expectation, more in line with a therapist as a kind of friend, has probably become more prevalent over recent decades.

Clients' expectations can be broken down into what they anticipate *will* happen and what they *wish* to happen. It seems that when given a choice and then offered their preferred option, they are fifty per cent less likely to drop out of therapy early on (McLeod, 2012). As the UK survey (cited above) has shown, many people are sceptical about the helpfulness of therapy. They may put their faith instead in physical exercise, complementary therapy, or simply struggling on. When clients arrive for an initial consultation, a therapist usually explores their previous experiences of help, their current preferences, and how they think therapy would work for them. If each problem is unique, and there is never just one ideal solution to it, it makes sense for a therapist to adopt a pluralistic approach. Therapy is much more likely to be successful when there is a good match between what clients want and what they receive (McLeod, 2013).

How do clients experience therapy?

There are many autobiographical accounts of the experience of being in therapy. Although this literature is a very interesting to read, it is too diverse to summarise here, and I will concentrate instead on published research.

A good way to obtain a clear idea of how therapy is experienced is to conduct in-depth interviews. Krause and colleagues (Krause et al., 2011; Krause, Altimir & Horvath, 2011) interviewed clients and therapists with the aim of comparing their experiences. The results showed that both parties emphasised the importance of an emotional bond. Clients expected therapists to be gentle, accepting, non-judgmental, warm, and empathic. This influenced their decision to remain in therapy after the first session. However, clients trod carefully, and many challenged the therapist to demonstrate her competence, at least initially. Once any resistance had been overcome, clients viewed the relationship as an intimate one but different in kind from any other relationship. The main differences were an expectation of expertise and an assurance of confidentiality. A therapist was "a very special friend" (Krause, Altimir

& Horvath, 2011, p. 272). Therapists also stressed the emotional bond and felt that their affection for a client was a good sign. They acknowledged the importance of sincerity and their need to be sensitive to a client's experiences and needs. In return, they expected a commitment from the client to themselves as people, as well as to the therapy.

The most notable differences in perception between clients and therapists in this study related to the former placing greater stress on expertise and years of experience, and the latter giving more emphasis to a client's commitment and collaboration. Seen from either perspective, their collaboration was a two-way interaction that could not be separated from the process of change. Of course, the relationship is asymmetric in the sense that a client is not helping a therapist to be accepted and understood. Nevertheless, apart from any progress made, clients increasingly valued therapists' emotional expressions towards them and "feeling close". The findings of this study are consistent with other research into the qualities of therapists that clients appreciate. These are flexibility, warmth, openness, respect, experience, trust, being encouraging, etc. (Ackerman & Hilsenroth, 2003; Henkelman & Paulson, 2006).

In a study of long-term mainly psychodynamic therapy, clients and therapists rated the quality of their relationship as it changed over time, in some cases over 120 sessions (Hersoug, Høgland, Havik, von der Lippe & Monson, 2009). For clients, a favourable rating of the relationship was determined chiefly by the strength of the emotional bond and the amount of collaboration over goals and tasks. This was less true for therapists. Therapists were asked to rate themselves on a questionnaire of interpersonal characteristics and their answers revealed that, compared to people in the general population, they were more "distanced, disconnected or indifferent". The higher these scores (and the more professional training a therapist had received) the more poorly the clients rated the quality of the relationship and the working alliance. It seems that clients prefer a warm and responsive therapist, and professional training does not seem to promote this.

In another study, the researchers interviewed eighteen clients after receiving a course of therapy (CBT for an anxiety problem) with a view to discovering how it was perceived (Westra, Aviram, Barnes & Angus, 2010). Nine clients had had a good outcome and nine a poor. For the majority, their experience of therapy did not conform to their expectations. They were either pleasantly surprised or disappointed. The former group welcomed the fact that the style of therapy was warm, collaborative, and non-judgemental, and they were surprised that therapy could be so helpful. For some, the process of therapy did not fit their stereotype (e.g., lying on a couch). The disappointed clients rarely blamed a therapist, feeling that they could have done more themselves to make it work. Despite disappointment, some clients thought it had not been a waste of time.

There are bound to be times when a therapist acts in such a way as to disappoint a client. Something might be said or done that is upsetting and this gets in the way of an effective working relationship. In order to avoid these ruptures, therapists are advised not to "mind-read" their clients, to check frequently with them for feedback, and not to rely too heavily on their own assumptions. Despite inevitable hiccups or setbacks, researchers have found that clients are rather reluctant to talk about having been dissatisfied or having had a bad experience (Henkelman & Paulson, 2006). They are much more willing to talk about what has been helpful. Perhaps this can be understood as an effect of being in a personal helping relationship as distinct from an impersonal contractual arrangement with a service provider. In other words, if a therapist has good intentions, it may seem unreasonable for a client to criticise. Once a client is committed to a therapist who is supporting her desire to change, to make much of a disappointing episode could hinder a process that is perceived, overall, as beneficial (Lietaer, 1992). By contrast, if a plumber does a bad job, one feels at liberty to complain loudly and insist on matters being put right immediately. A reluctance to express dissatisfaction with a therapist may explain why many clients unilaterally terminate their therapy without discussing this beforehand (a phenomenon that has been called "dropping out").

Why do clients "drop out"?

On the face of it, terminating therapy prematurely is a sign of dissatisfaction. Around one in five clients drop out before a therapist thinks it desirable (Swift & Greenberg, 2012). Clients may not inform their therapists of their decision to quit because they find it difficult to give critical feedback (Rhodes, Hill, Thompson & Elliott, 1994) or to say that they have not progressed as well as they would have hoped. For these clients, a therapist may not have sufficiently explored their aims or might have set higher goals than a client judged to be desirable or achievable. However, it would be incorrect to interpret all quitters as dissatisfied.

In one study of clients who terminated prematurely and later followed up with a telephone call, it was found that a proportion of them felt that they had already achieved their goals. However, for only a half of this group their therapists had realised this to be the case (Hunsley, Aubry, Vestervelt & Vito, 1999).

Clients who enter therapy have usually contemplated making a change but may still not be ready to put it into effect (Prochaska & DiClemente, 1992). In any case, clients might decide, after experience of therapy, that they would prefer a different approach. Swift and Greenberg (2012) found that premature termination was higher with certain kinds of problem (disorders of eating and severe difficulties in interpersonal relationships) but did not vary by type of therapy (e.g., psychodynamic or cognitive behavioural therapy). Clients were more likely to drop out when a therapist was a trainee or young. Of course, a therapist may lack the personal qualities a client is looking for. Apparently, a majority of clients expect therapy to last no longer than five sessions (Swift, Greenberg, Whipple & Kominiak, 2012), but in reality a longer duration is often needed.

When a client quits without explanation, a therapist may be left wondering what went wrong. It has been supposed that therapists can feel abandoned or betrayed, as well as disappointed. Farber (1983) had found that premature termination was the third greatest source of stress for a therapist, after a threat of suicide and hostility. In a study by Piselli, Halgin, and MacEwan (2011), eleven experienced therapists were asked to give an account of a memorable example and to reflect on their role in bringing it about. They found that the therapists thought it was something about the nature of a client's problem that had led them to drop out. In part, they believed that clients had other conflicting family or external difficulties; were not ready or willing to change; were easily hurt, angered, or dissatisfied; or that the therapist had not been able to establish a good working relationship. The therapists sometimes admitted to having been burned out, frustrated, or over-cautious. They also blamed themselves for being ineffective or for making mistakes. They experienced a variety of negative emotions when a client quit but, on the whole, the event did not affect their sense of competence. They had lingering regrets and wondered what they could have done differently to avert the outcome.

In the next chapter, I examine the evidence for the effectiveness of self-help. Perhaps there is no need for a therapist at all.

CHAPTER NINE

Do-it-yourself (DIY) therapy

In historical perspective, people have sought advice from books and mutual aid societies going back many centuries. Erudite discussion of how to live wisely and healthily has ancient origins. Present-day exhortations of a similar nature still have mass appeal. Do-it-yourself (DIY) therapy falls on a continuum with philosophy, religion, and entertainment. When therapy is seen as problem-solving rather than treatment of a disorder, the boundary between therapy and other ways of responding to life's challenges becomes very blurred indeed.

As technology advanced, advice from books was supplemented by telephone communication, newspaper agony columns, and later on still, by audio and video cassettes. These were followed by CDs and DVDs. The channels for advice have now mushroomed following the introduction of the internet and smartphone (I will refer to advice acquired through digital communication as e-therapy). Self-help books remain popular and constitute a highly profitable market for publishers. Television chat shows, reality programmes, and national celebrities have transformed other people's problems into entertainment (Wilson, 2003).

For mental health providers and policymakers, the internet has opened up enticing new possibilities for supplying a flexible service at low cost. Face-to-face therapy is undeniably expensive but with a modest investment of support supplied by a professional, clients can be offered self-help books or computerised learning materials and left to implement change themselves. The professional is there to select materials and guide a client when necessary. This can be done over the phone, by email or text, or through a website with interactive capabilities. One argument for developing these enhanced forms of DIY therapy is that access to professional help is very unevenly distributed across the country, and even for the services that do exist, there are long waiting lists. DIY therapy is a much cheaper alternative. Some people do fund therapy out of their own pocket, and for short or medium-term therapy, the cost of doing so is probably not much greater than the annual expense of servicing a car. However, the cost is clearly out of the reach of many.

In one sense, self-help is always a component of therapy. Clients translate ideas and exercises into practical action on their own initiative. Some therapists would describe what they do as facilitated self-help. Their role might be to help a client analyse the source of a problem, brainstorm a solution, and then prompt, encourage, and support its implementation. I frequently supplement therapy with educational material and/or exercises to be performed between sessions. In other words, there is no sharp division between DIY and face-to-face therapy. Email and the mobile phone also offer a rapid means of recording observations and reporting back on progress. One client of mine, whom I asked to record situations that evoked certain emotional reactions, would capture the situation with the camera on his smartphone (as a prompt for memory) and then, at the first opportunity, make an audio recording (also on his phone) of his immediate thoughts and feelings. He learned a great deal in this way without necessarily having to discuss it with me.

Some clients opt for self-help (or doing nothing) because they dislike putting themselves in the position of a help-seeker, which they may see as a sign of being weak-willed. To change customary habits and, heaven forbid, one's personality, is commonly resisted. In fact, when a client welcomes therapy too enthusiastically, it may turn out to be a trap to prove their therapist impotent.

The policymaker's perspective

If guided self-help could prove itself to be as effective as face-to-face therapy, it would clearly be welcomed. Some agencies that provide a mental health service use self-help as the first level in a programme of what is called stepped-care. Step zero is complete self-reliance, working alone from supplied materials. Step one is the provision of information, a book, CD, or piece of software, with some additional support. The steps above this supply varying degrees of guidance, either by means of telephone contact or through communication mediated by the internet. If necessary, supplementary face-to-face sessions can be arranged. Regular contact with a client is normally maintained by email, text message, message board, or by videoconferencing. Written messages can take a synchronous form (i.e., "chatting") or be asynchronous, in which case the advice seeker and therapist guide have time to reflect on what they want to say in reply to an earlier message. At the most intensive level of service in stepped provision, medium to long-term face-to-face or group therapy is offered. In this way, the most expensive service is restricted to people thought to be in most need of it.

An advantage of DIY therapy is that people living in areas too remote to have easy access to a professional can receive a service without incurring heavy costs in time and travel. Moreover, a problem may require specialist guidance and this may not be available locally. DIY therapy is also suited to people with limited mobility. It has the advantage of relative anonymity, obviating any embarrassment that might be felt in a face-to-face encounter with someone they know in a small-town setting. Furthermore, when communication is indirect, clients sometimes disclose more openly and honestly.

There is a weak link in the argument that stepped care, beginning with low-cost interventions, ultimately saves costs for healthcare providers. The weakness depends on the effectiveness of the early steps. If, let us say, only one half of clients feel that their problem has been resolved, this still leaves a half registered with the system who may demand to be stepped up to a more intensive and expensive level. In other words, attempts to provide an equitable and easily accessed lower-level service may ultimately increase demand for a higher-level service. An analogous example would be the availability of cheap foreign travel to relatively nearby locations, which seems to have fed a desire for more costly travel to distant and exotic locations.

Widespread public use of the internet has led to a considerable amount of experimentation into e-therapy. It has been offered to clients who are depressed, anxious, addicted to smoking, lonely, or who suffer poor sleep or have obsessional problems. This experimentation has not been motivated entirely by the promise of cost-savings. It is part of a wider development over the past century in which many traditional services and "crafts", including, for instance, the delivery of food, banking, and travel, have been rationalised. A service is broken down into simplified, uniform units, delivered in a standard way. In e-therapy, the client becomes a consumer abstracted from their social context, and she assumes responsibility for carrying out many of the components that define the service.

Reflecting back on a number of clients I have seen who had severe difficulties in their personal relationships, particularly when they related to historical abuse or emotional deprivation, I doubt that any of them would have entertained the idea of e-therapy. In fact, the offer of short-term or even medium-term face-to-face therapy would have been rejected as well. This would not have been an expression of neediness or dependency but a rational assessment of what short-term therapy had failed to offer them in the past. Opening up memories of painful or traumatic experiences should not be attempted unless the consequences of doing so can be managed and successfully resolved. Many clients will only allow themselves to enter into this process once they have developed trust and confidence in their therapist. For many problems, e-therapy is not the solution.

Is guided self-help effective?

In order for a rationally managed service to function smoothly, its components have to be reduced to their bare essentials. It does not work if every consumer comes with a problem that is uniquely related to their individual circumstances. Consequently, researchers into the effectiveness of guided self-help have followed the strategy of standardisation that I outlined in previous chapters; this usually means defining a problem in terms of criteria set out in psychiatric diagnostic manuals. The primary measure of success then becomes a reduction in "symptoms". These uniform scales for measuring symptoms and quality of life provide little information about a person's total life situation before and after therapy. For instance, an equivalent reduction of depressed mood after guided self-help and pharmacotherapy would not tell you that, in the former case, a client's increased sense of well-being led her to leave her long-term partner, and that in the latter case, one of the side-effects of medication was sexual dysfunction. This can occur in between twenty-five and eighty per cent of clients who take an antidepressant (Serretti & Chiesa, 2009).

Looking on the optimistic side, research into guided self-help has shown that clients often rate it as no less satisfactory than face-to-face therapy, and the results it achieves compare favourably (Richards & Viganó, 2013). There are, however, reasons to be cautious. A research study requires potential participants to jump through various hoops before they can be selected, and so the results may not apply to a wider population. For example, when computerised therapy was offered to clients who were waiting to receive publicly provided face-to-face therapy, fifty-six per cent of them dropped out of the study, and seventy-three per cent of those who engaged with it did not complete all five e-therapy modules (Twomey et al., 2014). Any evaluation of e-therapy should therefore take account of how many people were excluded, declined it, or failed to finish it.

Another reason to be cautious is that researchers may be over-generous when interpreting their own results. As we saw in Chapter Six, approximately one quarter of clients seem to be "early responders" who perhaps are ready and open to change and just need prompting into making it. One study of online therapy for panic attacks and a fear of public places (agoraphobia) illustrates the point that this kind of help may only skim off a minority of clients as clear "successes" (Kiropoulos et al., 2008). The participants, who were predominantly professional people with internet access, were recruited from the community. One randomly selected group received an online manualised programme of CBT with prompt asynchronous email contacts for feedback and support. A second group received twelve weekly sessions of face-to-face therapy that employed a similar manualised CBT approach but with individually tailored assistance from their therapist. As the authors state, seventy-five to ninety-five per cent of clients in previous studies of face-to-face therapy have reached panic-free status at the end of therapy. This benefit is usually maintained for up to two years. Kiropoulos and colleagues obtained panic-free status for only around thirty-five per cent of clients in each of their groups, with a somewhat lower proportion than this classified as achieving what they called high end-state functioning. The participants were not reassessed at a follow-up and so even these changes may not have been long-lasting. It seems clear that if seventy-five to ninety-five per cent is the accepted going rate for success, the sixty-five per cent of participants in this study who did not reach it are likely to want to be "stepped up" for more intensive therapy. Moreover, clients who do not have the advantages of the high level of education of the participants in this study may not even reach the thirty-five per cent success rate obtained with this selected group.

A recent overview of fifty-six articles on self-help therapy clarifies some of the factors that have a bearing on success (Haug, Nordgreen, Ost & Havik, 2012). The articles reported the results of self-help therapy with eight different types of anxiety problem. Overall, e-therapy was considerably more helpful than simply remaining on a waiting list. It was also superior to receiving a placebo (dummy) therapy. In general, clients recruited from the community benefited more than those who had already been referred to a clinical service. Rather surprisingly, guided self-help was not noticeably more effective than pure self-help, which hardly supports the need for a professional. As the authors remark: "In the research literature on psychotherapy outcome, the quality of the therapeutic relationship is usually seen as the most important common factor in psychological treatments and has consistently been found to be associated with treatment outcome" (ibid., p. 441). In a similar review of e-therapy, Farrand and Woodford (2013) found that the type of guidance offered made no difference (apart from telephone support, which produced somewhat better results).

However, Haug and colleagues found that the results of e-therapy were not quite as good as face-to-face therapy. Moreover, in a later investigation of face-to-face therapy for anxiety problems (based on a manualised version of CBT) Haug (2014) reported that therapists' competence and their ability to establish a good working alliance was related to the results they obtained. Bearing in mind the findings of all the various reviews just mentioned, the quality and type of human contact does seem to make a difference. However, it is far less important than one might expect.

Haug and colleagues (2012) found that face-to-face contact showed the greatest advantage for overcoming specific phobias and post-traumatic stress. Specific phobias are generally the easiest anxiety problem to resolve successfully. However, it is unlikely that a person with, say, a fear of enclosed places or spiders, would find it easy to self-administer a programme of exposure to these situations without guidance and encouragement. With skilled help and the reassuring presence of another person in the feared situation, a phobia can usually be overcome fairly rapidly. The benefits of face-to-face therapy are likely to greatly outweigh its costs, given its brevity and effectiveness. It hardly seems necessary to promote a cheaper alternative that may be less effective.

For readers who may be interested, the following references review the evidence for e-therapy applied to some common problems: anxiety (ibid.), depression (Richards & Richardson, 2012), eating disorders (Loucas et al., 2014), insomnia (Ho et al., 2014); obsessions (Herbst et al., 2012).

What is e-therapy like?

A published case study illustrates the way that e-therapy works in an established service (Pugh, Hadjistavropoulos, Klein & Austin, 2014). Potential clients first undergo a telephone screening interview which asks them about their life circumstances and establishes a psychiatric diagnosis (in the client whose case is described, this was depression and generalised anxiety disorder). The therapist is either a fully trained clinical psychologist or a psychologist in training. Confidentiality is ensured by encrypting personal identifying information and storing it securely. The subject of the case study was a retired man in a stable marriage, who had had many previous episodes of depression. He was offered a programme that consisted of twelve interactive modules, including text, graphics, and animation, in audio and video format. The modules covered topics such as psychoeducation, behavioural activation, healthy lifestyle, and thinking styles.

The client's understanding of the material and his mood were monitored weekly. Exercises were assigned, to be carried out between online sessions, and the therapist composed a weekly feedback review sent by email. Over the course of twenty-one weeks, he received twenty emails from his therapist and spoke once over the telephone when he failed to check in as expected. His understanding and use of the material elicited replies from his therapist designed to bolster hope, reinforce insight, build an alliance, and reflect back on his thoughts and feelings. The therapist's comments (of which many examples are provided in the article) sound rather formulaic. Their content is possibly sufficiently predictable to be programmed into a computer, for example, "Thanks for being so honest," "It is great [in bold text] that you recognised that your past activities were primarily achievement-focused," "It was nice to read that you found my email encouraging." The client also responded to specific questions that his therapist posed to him.

At the end of the course of therapy he expressed his appreciation: "It is surprising how a few understanding and encouraging words from someone can be such a help." He commented that he had been accepted "for who I was" and "I still find it hard to believe that I was able to share my thoughts and feelings with you."

As the authors of the article note, the therapist often began her emails with informal chat (e.g. "How was your weekend?") and this may have done much to simulate a friendship-like relationship. They also observe that the therapist kept to the confines of the modular (educational) material and did not inquire further when the client made remarks that would normally have been followed up in face-to-face therapy. For instance, he wrote that thinking of his mother had triggered feelings of guilt, and that one module aroused painful childhood memories. It may not have been critical to investigate these "pointers" but, in my experience, it is rare for therapy to proceed down a predictable track, having begun with a clear identification and formulation of the presenting problem. In the case of this particular client, he responded well to some general therapeutic principles and exercises. However, it seems likely that significant problems will occasionally be missed with this shotgun approach. A key statement from this client at the termination of therapy was as follows: "I believe that I was ready to put my heart and soul into this program when I began. This was probably because I had tried medications and one-on-one counselling with minimal success in the past." The timing of the intervention seems to have been crucial; he had reached a moment in life when he was ready to make a change.

Guided self-help and friendship

Communication in e-therapy is indirect, and in this way it differs from face-to-face therapy. A voice or written word coming from a technical device does not provide as many cues as a live person. There is also no "healing setting", with its books and its diplomas on the wall. However, if therapy really does depend on the cultivation of a form of friendship, this should not matter too much. Distance has never been a problem in the past. The ancient Egyptians, Greeks, and Romans maintained their friendships through endearing letters, and letter writing continued to serve this function until it was all but extinguished by email and texting.

One of the downsides is that the anonymity of internet communication creates opportunities for deception, impression management, disinhibition, and unethical behaviour (Richards & Viganó, 2013). Moreover, when contact is remote, it may not be possible to act effectively if a client is in extreme distress or expressing suicidal intent. E-therapy is therefore unsuitable for problems such as domestic violence or historical child abuse. In some cases, a therapist's license to practise is limited to a certain geographical area, and legal responsibilities may differ between areas as well. Professional organisations have developed ethical guidelines for this type of practice.

The twin facts that e-therapists are appreciated by their clients and that they can achieve good results, calls into question the great importance that some researchers have attached to the quality of the therapy relationship in face-to-face therapy (Peck, 2010). Is a strong bond really so necessary or can the grounds for this assumption be explained differently? The comments cited above, made by the man who received e-therapy, rather suggest that the whole process was a virtual one, in which the therapist was not a real person but a composite of his imagination. It is possible that the observed positive correlation between the strength of the therapy bond and the benefits obtained through therapy is also a product of a misplaced attribution to a "real" person. In other words, clients who are determined to change, and manage to do so, feel grateful to a therapist who cheers them on from the sidelines. They may attribute the positive results of their own efforts to the attachment they form with a therapist.

An alternative interpretation of the effectiveness of e-therapy is that the educational material supplied is capable of providing insight into the nature of a problem. It may also provide the tools that are necessary to solve it. The research evidence tends to show that a guiding hand from an actual professional produces a better outcome than pure self-help alone. This may be so because advice is needed to translate the educational advice into effective practice. However, as I commented earlier, indirect human contact can be a potent way of forming a close relationship. In a comparison between face-to-face and telephone therapy for depressed clients, no difference was found in the strength of the "working alliance" or in the effectiveness of therapy (Stiles-Shields, Kwasny, Cai & Mohr, 2014).

I am still rather doubtful that clients who know that they are communicating with a machine programmed to be "helpful" would find this as motivating as knowing that their communication is taking place with an actual person. According to the results of a study by

Talbot (2012), human contact that offered no guidance whatsoever added to the effectiveness of purely self-administered e-therapy. Perhaps, in a similar way, friends ask one another how they are getting along with a problem without wanting to know (or expecting to hear) any of the details. It is enough to know that someone else cares enough to ask.

CHAPTER TEN

Therapy as social regulation

Psychotherapy has attracted a great deal of social and political comment and this is not surprising. Taken together with self-help literature, the sale of DVDs, and workshops, therapy is a large sector of the economy. If therapy is a socially sanctioned form of friendship (at least in part), we could say that a naturally available form of advice, support and counsel has been transformed into a saleable commodity within a capitalist economy. As Paul Wachtel (1977, p. 289) points out, the new personal services emphasise "change from within", and so they are compatible with the individualistic spirit of Western culture. For instance, the ethical stance of humanistic and psychoanalytic therapy is not to influence a client directly by suggesting a structured course of action. The client must work it out alone as if a pioneer battling with the elements.

A hands-off attitude could deny a client the practical advice and support that would normally be available if therapy were to be more closely modelled on friendship. Some therapies, such as CBT, do stress the collaborative nature of the relationship and the reciprocity of joint problem-solving. However, in other respects, therapy is similar to any other consumer service. It involves a direct or indirect financial transaction, which means that a certain amount of control over the aims and type of service can be exerted by the payer. The only forms of therapy that do not compete in a consumer marketplace are those that are conducted voluntarily, often in leaderless groups. They may seek to exert a broad social/political influence, for instance, by transforming negative stereotypes or by introducing new models of intervention, for example, the Hearing Voices Movement (James, 2001).

Therapy is inherently political because it is one of the ways in which behaviour is socially regulated. Nikolas Rose spelled this out in his book *Governing the Soul* (Rose, 1989). Therapy aims to help people to function autonomously and to refashion their self in a preferred direction. Rose believes it promotes adherence to social norms, especially when a client internalises therapeutic principles as a form of self-management. A client may also be motivated to conform to an image of happy and successful selves presented in the media. Their very existence invites self-scrutiny and an effort to match the ideal, prompting a tendency to turn to a therapist to assist with the necessary reskilling and personality change. The widespread adoption of assertiveness training since the late 1940s must have encouraged people to argue for their rights in domestic and work situations with an effect, however difficult to measure, on social norms. Trainers in assertiveness sometimes refer to the *United Nations' Universal Declaration of Human Rights* that includes the right to freedom of opinion and expression. Rose seems to hint that there is something sinister about normative self-regulation through the medium of advice and therapy but what the negative nature of this influence might be is rather unclear.

Other sociologists are more forthcoming. Eva Illouz thinks that psychology's "cultural impact should worry us" (Illouz, 2008, p. 247). She believes there has been a major shift in how people are regulated over the past 100 years, in part resulting from the influence of theories and practices of psychologists and psychotherapists. I examine her arguments below.

The existence of a political dimension to therapy is obvious in two other senses. First, there is a relationship between the amount of psychological suffering and a person's class, gender, ethnicity, employment status, and other social characteristics. The state provision of therapy is one way of responding to inequalities or social disadvantage by attempting to ameliorate them. Second, people have come to feel that they have a right to help with personal problems, and governments seek legitimacy through providing services, including therapy, that aim to reduce hardship and suffering.

If we really wanted to investigate the political dimension of therapy on a micro scale, it could be done by studying audio or video-recorded sessions of actual therapy. We could then see what kind of behaviour and attitudes were being encouraged or discouraged. However, one of the first rules of the therapy professions is confidentiality. A therapist could be struck off if found to be discussing a client in sufficient detail for them to be publicly identified. Case studies are published in an anonymous, cleaned up, and reconstructed form. Supervisors and trainers have access to what actually happens in therapy but they are bound by the rule of confidentiality as well. Any written record of a session is required to be placed in a locked filing cabinet or, if stored digitally, should be password protected. In the UK, a therapist should register with the government's Data Controller. Although personal material can be studied or published in an anonymous form, there is rather little research that reveals the micro-political processes taking place during therapy.

Styles of therapy vary greatly, and it is not easy to identify their value judgements or political content. For instance, it would be interesting, though difficult, to trace the origins and impact of recent enthusiasm for oriental techniques of meditation. Some sociologists believe that psychological theory and practice influences society in a unique way. For them, the direction of causality is mostly one way, from psychology and psychotherapy to society. In reality, therapy has always absorbed external influences. Some techniques in CBT resemble the management practices of large institutions and businesses, which have only a tenuous connection with psychological theory. Clients may be asked to manage their lives by writing down a list of goals, audit their resources, assess risks, develop skills, implement decisions, and monitor feedback on progress. This type of problem-solving is found in many areas of life, and although psychologists undoubtedly contributed to its development, it would be too easy to attribute modern management practices primarily to them.

The public lacks knowledge of what actually takes place in therapy and so it has been left in a state of ignorance or, worse, misinformation.

Autobiographical accounts are illuminating but they are almost invariably retrospective reconstructions which may refer to events in an earlier historical period. The public image of the therapist seems to have been created largely by film, television, cartoonists, and comedians. Sociological critiques are undertaken by authors who are not therapists themselves, and they may have had no personal experience as a consumer. If psychologists and therapists had really exerted such a profound and pervasive influence on society, one would expect members of the public to be able to differentiate the roles of psychiatrist, psychotherapist, psychoanalyst, clinical psychologist, and counsellor. In fact, it is rare to find anyone who can do so. For instance, Illouz (2008) confuses the American Psychological Association with the American Psychiatric Association.

A reluctance to produce records and transcripts of therapy sessions may come from therapists themselves. A session cannot be an entirely pre-planned event, and even when a therapist is following a manual, the unpredictable often occurs. For this reason, a session is like a piece of improvised theatre. A therapist has to be alert and quick thinking, but given the need to pay attention to so many things at once (building trust, providing information, attending to one's thoughts as well as to a client's responses), there are bound to be examples of false starts, mishandled questions, embarrassing silences, and the like. On hearing or seeing a recorded session, a therapist will be struck by lapses of attention and moments of losing the plot.

In exceptional circumstances, therapy concerns itself explicitly with moral questions and political issues. Clients may be helped to become aware of the ways in which they are tacitly acting in accordance with values and norms that they have come to question (see, for example, Law, 1999). Clients commonly discuss parental precepts and cultural assumptions, not because they are necessarily inimical to leading a satisfactory life, but because the clients no longer have any use for them and want to challenge their influence. It is not so much a question of a therapist imposing new values or political opinions as a client coming to realise a source of dissatisfaction that was only previously half-intuited. A therapist might, however, take the lead in encouraging a client to question assumptions that appear to be having an oppressive effect, such as a psychiatric label, or a social class or gender stereotype. Discussion may focus on the familial and cultural sources of a client's sense of identity and, where appropriate, clients are encouraged to make deliberate attempts to change their way of life. This is political activity in a small p sense.

Psychotherapy and the transformation of traditional society

Of major interest to sociologists is the way that society has changed as a result of the decline in religious authority, a reduction in coercive methods of social control, and, to a large degree, by freedom from the constraints of poverty and hunger. Accompanying these social trends, traditional formulaic ethical notions and rigid criteria for truth have been replaced by methods of reasoning that originated in science and the arts. People can use these intellectual tools to reflect on the meaning and direction their lives are taking. A consideration of all these historical trends has led to the thesis that people are not so much controlled by external authorities as control themselves by choosing what kind of person they want to be (Elchardus, 2009).

There are two ways of understanding this transformation. The first is to suppose that people have become more reflexive in planning their lives through their adoption of disciplined methods of reasoning and self-management. The second is that people have merely been persuaded to think of themselves as autonomous choosing agents. If emphasis is given to the latter interpretation, it may be argued that they have been manoeuvred by government policies, advertising, the media, therapy, etc., to imagine that they can regulate themselves, whereas, in reality, control lies elsewhere. In other words, social control is exercised by forces that mould the factors that determine choice. Mark Elchardus notes that the humanistic psychology of Carl Rogers denies any need for external social control because "desirable order emerges spontaneously from the actions of autonomous individuals able to be authentic, true to their selves" (ibid., p. 156). Critics of Rogers' point of view would argue that this is a fiction that conceals and promotes a different form of (external) social control.

Therapy has therefore been attacked for creating the idea that persons can or should view themselves as choosing agents. Traditionalists argue that self-fashioning can become an obsession with selfish needs and, consequently, that "therapy culture" undermines traditional values of resilience, forbearance, and personal accountability. People who seek therapy when they confront an obstacle to meeting their needs are seen as weak-willed, especially when their "failure" triggers distressing emotions that they perceive as being "not their own fault". In this way, therapy is thought to encourage victimhood and dependence on welfare. The critic may go on to argue that the welfare state should be rolled back to expose people to the realities of life with which they will have to come to terms without the benefit of illness labels or support for their "vulnerability".

From an opposite perspective, it is argued that the growth in popularity of therapy simply shows that the individual is being duped (and controlled) into taking responsibility for personal problems, blame for which should really be placed elsewhere in society. The individual fails to see this because he is mystified by a belief that the meaning and course of his life should depend wholly on his own decisions. If he fails to match up to social expectations, he willingly accepts an illness label. He may indeed think he is in need of therapy because he has a disorder. For instance, a person's depressed mood is attributed to his illness of depression rather than to his state of unemployment or social isolation.

One feature of modern life that these analyses rarely mention is the vastly increased number of choices that people want to make, or feel compelled to make. Cheap international travel (as well as the media) has exposed people to alternative beliefs and lifestyles. New technologies, such as the world wide web, give people instant access to the store of the world's knowledge and the possibility of intimate contact with complete strangers. People may not be able to resist viewing themselves as choosing agents simply because there are so many more options to choose from. Internet dating now allows people in time-consuming and/or isolating jobs (e.g., 18-hour-a-day city workers or farmers in remote locations) to make contacts quickly and easily. It is hardly surprising that people take advantage of these technical innovations. For instance, why be stoical about one's hearing impairment now that highly sophisticated hearing aids and cochlear implants are available? Nevertheless, many people do put up with not hearing well (or at all) on grounds of stoically "having to put up with it" as an inevitable effect of aging. It would be more rational to take advantage of the available technologies. On similar grounds, it is hardly selfish to seek out psychological techniques that can produce rapid change in debilitating psychological problems such as panic attacks, phobias, stuttering, or obsessions. People in all historical (and probably pre-historical) periods have taken up new technological innovations regardless of how they perceived themselves as agents.

A counter-argument to a welcoming attitude to technical advance and expanding opportunity is that people now expect a degree of self-realisation that is actually unattainable, and that this brings suffering in its wake. However, it has not been my experience as a therapist that clients expect too much. Rather, they want the normal satisfactions that others have. Reviewing the problems presented by my last ten clients, all of them amount to the removal of blocks and obstacles to everyday functioning. They include dealing with the breakdown of an intimate relationship, with the consequences of road traffic accidents, with anxiety about public speaking, with fluctuating mood, with concern about bodily appearance, with anger control, and with difficulties in social relationships. These are not selfish or overambitious concerns in the normal sense of the word. If everyone has raised expectations and most people manage to meet them, we can hardly condemn individuals who try to shape up and match the norm. In any case, many clients seek therapy because of the consequences of their problem on others.

There appears to have been an exponential rise in the frequency with which people seek advice from therapists of all kinds. In a nationwide survey conducted in the US in 1960 that investigated who it was that people turned to for help when they had a psychological problem, forty-two per cent said the clergy, twenty-nine per cent their doctor, twelve per cent a psychiatrist or psychologist, ten per cent other forms of counselling or therapy, six per cent lawyers, and the remainder other agencies (Bergin, 1971, p. 243). In 1994, 7,000 readers of the magazine *Consumer Reports* who had "experienced stress or emotional problems in the previous three years" responded to a request to fill in a questionnaire asking them about where and from whom they had sought help (Seligman, 1995). Of these, forty-two per cent had sought advice only from friends, relatives or clergy (the latter now relegated to non-professional status). Fifty-eight per cent had seen a combination of mental health professionals, psychologists being the most frequently consulted (37%). In addition, fourteen per cent had seen a family physician and eighteen per cent had joined a self-help group. Although a direct comparison cannot be made, it seems that fifty-five years on, members of the clergy and physicians are no longer the first port of call for help.

I will now examine some critiques of therapy from the right and left wings of political opinion.

Critiques from the right

Eva Illouz

In her book *Saving the Modern Soul: Therapy, Emotions, and the Culture of Self-help* (2008), Illouz's main message is a moral one. She believes that therapy encourages people to play the victim role, allowing them to avoid taking responsibility for their actions. The scope of her review goes far beyond face-to-face therapy because she discusses a broad swathe of psychologists, self-appointed gurus, and popular writers who focus on emotional communication. Nevertheless, she attributes a major cultural shift to "the world view of a particular class of professionals—the psychologists—who have historically been extraordinarily successful in claiming a monopoly over the definition and the rules of emotional life in the private and public spheres" (ibid., p. 210).

Illouz believes that it was Freud and psychoanalysis that largely brought about this significant change in Western culture. According to Illouz, his ideas heralded a focus on banal everyday phenomena, such as dreams and slips of the tongue, and on the pathology of the nuclear family from which a person had to be liberated. A search for the "sense" of a symptom invited everyone to become interpreters of their own life. Positive mental health was seen as the endpoint of therapy, as the person acquired self-knowledge through rational means. According to Illouz, psychotherapy, beginning at the latter end of the nineteenth century, has developed into a "therapeutic discourse" which "has become a cultural form shaping and organizing experience" (ibid., p. 56). Illouz suggests that "this [therapeutic] language has virtually no antecedent in American or European culture" (ibid., p. 5).

Although it is true to say that Freud had a huge influence, an untold number of "experts" on the human condition have spread their ideas, and psychoanalysis is only one of them. The experimental psychologists, Ivan Pavlov, J. B. Watson, and B. F. Skinner were the chief inspiration for behaviour therapy, and this was a very different kind of therapy discourse. In any case, if such a discourse exists, it can hardly be attributed to psychologists' extraordinarily successful quest for power or the fact that they have become powerful legislators of various domains of social life. This would be rather like attributing the spread of Marxism to Marx's personal quest for power. It psychologises a social phenomenon.

As I have argued in previous chapters, the form that helpful advice and wise counsel take includes the way that questions are asked, the values that guide the encounter, the limits placed on confidentiality, and norms relating to disclosure. If these are part of "therapy culture", they have a very ancient origin. As a unique and new form of help, psychotherapy was embedded in a process beginning much earlier in the nineteenth century when human misery was medicalised. This takeover began when the care of the mad by "moral managers" was transferred to physicians running large asylums (Boyle, 2002). These also dealt with the poor and destitute who might formerly have been helped by the parish or placed in a workhouse. The word "therapy" bears witness to its medical origins. However, ideas of self-improvement can be traced back to much earlier periods. The growth of counselling as a profession has also been an example of a trend towards redefining advice and problem-solving outside the scope of medical concepts of therapy and disorder.

Illouz believes that therapy discourse "removes any notion of moral culpability", that "suffering has been transformed into victimhood", and that "an identity status as a victim is acquired in the very act of telling others one's injuries in public" (ibid, p. 184). This portrayal of clients does not correspond at all with my experience as a therapist. Clients typically tell of their injuries without imputing victimhood to themselves. In fact, it is more likely to be the case that a client sees herself as morally culpable without any conceivable justification. Perhaps Illouz's views stem from the idea that people who are tough, morally strong, and resourceful do not become victims. One wonders how she would view the men and women who have come forward to report having been abused, sexually and physically, by priests and media celebrities. Does this courageous telling of past events in a public court amount to embracing the victim role? In my experience, clients, like everyone else, wrestle with problems and moral dilemmas which they feel they have a duty to sort out. Entering therapy is hard work and does not, for them, offer any advantage of victim status. The adoption of an illness label in order to profit is not unknown but it seems to be no more common than fraudulently claiming for whiplash after a road traffic accident.

Frank Furedi

Frank Furedi's book *Therapy Culture* (2003) conveys a similar message to Illouz's, although his style is more polemical. He is not critical of therapeutic techniques as such but of the way the language and beliefs that underpin them have developed into what he calls a "cultural ethos", "a world view" or a "therapeutic imagination". He goes so far as to say that "arguably, it is the most important signifier of meaning for the everyday life of the individual" (ibid, p. 22). I am not sure how the range of possible everyday signifiers could be meaningfully assessed, compared, and ranked. As stated, Furedi's claim seems wild. His argument is that the therapeutic world view does the following things: (i) objectifies the uncertainties of life into risks, (ii) induces a sense of vulnerability, powerlessness, and helplessness, (iii) encourages the idea that people are in need of counselling in order to cope with ordinary emotional challenges, (iv) constitutes an outlook that "overwhelms more traditional codes of meaning" (ibid., p. 17), (v) "stigmatises informal relations of dependence" and produces "the disorganisation of the private sphere" (ibid., p. 21).

Furedi does not regard therapy culture to be an inevitable consequence of the transition from traditional to modern forms of life. However, he argues that governments can use therapy as an instrument for social control that "bypasses the resistance of the individual" and influences "their internal life" (ibid., p. 95). Given that therapy is voluntary, I presume that this can only be done indirectly by influencing the goals of therapy through the selective allocation of funds or by supporting certain public health messages and skills programmes (e.g., training in parenting skills). However, Furedi also suggests that the welfare state rewards people by permitting a diagnosis that allows them to play the sick role. According to him, the therapist is turned into an authority figure upon whom clients become dependent, rendering them receptive to manipulation of their internal lives. For instance, hostile impulses towards the social order could be deflected and defused. He argues that there are advantages to the individual of an illness identity, such as gaining access to a support network in the voluntary sector.

Like Illouz, Furedi believes that the illness role leads to a suspension of normal moral responsibilities, thereby eroding traditional codes of conduct. He associates the latter with stoicism, bravery, resilience, and sacrifice. As he argues, even the police and the military have embraced therapy culture through their acceptance of diagnoses such as post-traumatic stress disorder. He writes that in the past, "problems in the private sphere were best left to the informal solutions worked out by people in their communities" (ibid., p. 99). However, one wouldn't want to go back too far into the past to a period of witchcraft accusations, social ostracism, and widespread acceptance of wife-beating. Without empirical support, Furedi's sociological argument is little more than conjecture backed up by circulating opinions and news stories. As a moral standpoint, stoicism only makes sense when a problem cannot be changed. Perhaps therapy culture has stifled impulses to promote social change through traditional political mechanisms but I am not aware of evidence of this effect. It is a romantic notion to suppose that we can return to a time (if it ever existed) when the informal help provided by friends and communities was a sufficient resource to overcome personal suffering.

Some critiques from the left

David Smail

David Smail has written a steady stream of books but I will focus on *Power, Interest and Psychology* (2005) to represent his political position. His main message is that a person's motives, desires, sense of self, and agency are largely determined by environmental influences, especially power in all its material and non-material forms. People are said to be largely ignorant of this fact and can provide merely a "commentary" on their problems that helps very little when they want to change their lives. The aim of therapy should be "outsight" rather than insight, in order to demystify the causes of their suffering. People's commentary on themselves is largely "just talk" and their cognition and their will "seem incapable of affecting what they do or how they feel" (ibid., p. 45). He believes that personal faults or inadequacies are more accurately understood as "deficits within their social environment" (ibid., p. 38). This is more or less what the behaviourist B. F. Skinner would have argued (Skinner, 1973), but Smail has no time at all for his kind of analysis.

Smail's position is deeply contradictory. On the one hand "there is no such thing as an autonomous individual" (2005, p. 46) but on the other hand, the really powerful apparently choose to exert their power in order to mystify others. He thinks that psychology has played its part in this as well because "it has been fundamental to the creation of the perfect consumer in our capitalist society" (ibid., p. ii). To be consistent, Smail should say that we are all completely mystified by the forces that control us. The opposition he sets up is between a ruthlessly competitive social Darwinism and … well, what? Here he resorts to metaphor: "a culture adequate to the blooming of subjectivity" in which "the spirit may blossom and flourish" (ibid., p. iv). Who could disagree with those utopian aims? However, at this point, Smail has to resort to a notion of individual agency, or deliberate wilfulness, because this kind of world is, as he says, "an ethical choice" (ibid., p. v).

In my view, the constitution of individuals as agents who make ethical choices is itself a political ideology, one that developed with Renaissance Humanism and the Enlightenment. This ideology does at least permit the individual some influence over the world. To argue as Smail does that individuals merely mediate rather than originate change in the environment seems to presuppose that it is philosophically and scientifically tenable to argue for a sharp dichotomy between internal and external causation. We might want to argue about the extent to which individuals are allowed "real" choice within the present political system, and agree with Smail that too much is expected of "willpower". However, to believe that the individual is as powerless as Smail maintains would seem to be a counsel of despair, rendering therapy of little relevance. He is, however, willing to assign therapy a modest social role of comforting, encouraging, and clarifying people's problems.

For all its undoubted weaknesses, a culture that constructs the individual as an autonomous agent seems preferable to one that appeals to external authority, whether in the form of naked coercion or spiritual powers. The granting of personal autonomy is never absolute, and when responsibility is assigned, it usually takes account of overwhelming external influence. Social institutions, such as the judiciary, build this into their practices. Even the fifteenth-century Catholic priest John Mirc, when deciding on the magnitude of a sin and an appropriate penance, attempted a balanced assessment of self-control and the spiritual powers of God and the Devil (see Chapter Two). There is some room within therapy to encourage a client to free herself from the binding power of others, whether this takes the form of family members, friends, or social institutions.

Paul Moloney

I hesitate to place Paul Moloney on the Left because in his book *The Therapy Industry: The Irresistible Rise of the Talking Cure, and Why it Doesn't Work* (2013), he quotes approvingly from Illouz and Furedi. He shares their view that "therapy culture" within US and UK society encourages self-centredness and a false sense of personal vulnerability. He associates this with "a growth in surveillance of personal health, family life, and education by central government and their agencies" (ibid., p. 119. His political argument is that policy should focus instead on the social, material, and environmental conditions that are known to be correlated with human misery. The answer for him is prevention rather than cure. Therapy represents "little more than a comfort blanket for the practitioner and client alike" (ibid., p. 83). It doesn't work because people "are locked into tough or demoralising circumstances that do not admit change" (ibid., p. 3). According to him, therapy adjusts people to their circumstance. It is not clear whether Moloney believes that therapy would be unnecessary in a better designed society, or, if it was thought to be necessary, what it would set out to achieve.

The hypothesis that therapists adjust people to their oppressive environments could be researched but for it to gain support would take close analysis of what actually takes place in therapy sessions. An empirical investigation of this kind might help to explain why therapy sometimes proves useless or harmful. Its subtle political or regulatory functions could be examined. As far as I am aware, this kind of research is rare or non-existent.

Moloney's appraisal of the effectiveness of therapy is based on a review of the results of randomised control trials (RCTs). He concludes that they fail "to convincingly show that talking treatment works" (ibid., p. 90). However, it is unclear that he would *want* therapy to work if it adjusts people to their circumstances. He seems to accept the medical framework in which the research is conducted, itself part of a therapy culture that he ought to regard as a form of mystification. If the evidence for talking therapy is weak or non-existent, state funding should cease. The rich can indulge themselves with private therapy while the poor will be no worse off. However, if Moloney believes that the provision of therapy serves a different political purpose, that of adjusting people to their toxic material conditions, reinforcing the idea that individual citizens are responsible for their own suffering, its funding would be assured on this basis, regardless of its effectiveness. In fact, failing to provide it might lead people to select other solutions and perhaps expose the real material causes of misery that Moloney assumes to be causing suffering.

If the social/material causes of personal problems and unhappiness could be mitigated, this preventative strategy would still not do away with all human suffering. For instance, it seems impossible to prevent broken relationships and sexual abuse, even when there is a close (and sometimes unacceptably high) level of social surveillance. Moloney surely cannot be arguing that there is no place for the consolation and alleviation of suffering at an individual level.

Individual therapy does not limit itself to what is going on "inside a person's head". In a limited way, it can attend to some of the material and social systemic causes of individual problems. However, it is true that many forms of psychotherapy place little emphasis on formulating the unique determinants of a client's problem in a broad social context (Hallam, 2013a). This is one consequence of taking the easy option of identifying a problem by means of a psychiatric diagnosis. It takes time and effort to produce an individual formulation, and if the practice were to be adopted, it would complicate research and practice enormously. Despite its inherent complexity, there is a strong tradition of individual case formulation within therapy. A systemic and functional approach was developed early on by therapists such as Israel Goldiamond (Schwartz & Goldiamond, 1975) who was informed both by his experimental laboratory research and his work with clients. This approach to formulation pays particular attention to the environmental determinants of a problem, whether or not a client has noticed them or understood them to be significant. They are the public equivalent of Freud's unconscious region of the mind.

Moloney does an intellectual about turn when he approvingly discusses a detailed qualitative analysis of shame in people who had received treatment within the mental health system (Leeming, Boyle, & MacDonald, 2009). He comments by saying that "talking therapists should find better ways of helping people to understand how their troubles relate to their environment, and that 'failure to cope' need not equate with personal slippage, or blame." This remark seems to show that he underestimates what many therapists do routinely.

Having worked in several economically deprived areas of London, I am well aware that social adversity contributes heavily to personal problems. On the one hand, therapy adjusts people to their circumstances but, on the other hand, these are the conditions they are forced to live with anyway. Adjustment need not imply "giving in to". Therapy may do little more than take the edge off difficult social circumstances but sometimes clients will decide to make radical changes in their life. There is also nothing intrinsic to therapy that deters people from becoming social activists.

Therapy and social welfare

Therapy and counselling are provided at the state's expense on the understanding that there is a need to take care of "mental health" as well as physical health. There is clearly a responsibility to take care of people who put themselves or others at risk. When this happens, mental health law makes provision for involuntary management in hospital or in the community. However, the present UK Mental Health Act does not attempt to define mental illness. The words used are "a disorder of the mind". This tautology (mental disorder is a disorder of the mind) is an admission that the concept of mental illness is a myth, and this allows considerable slippage in deciding what legal powers are necessary. It is very difficult to create a sensible boundary between ordinary misery, so-called "mild conditions", and "mental illness" that requires social management. Whether someone presents a risk may have little to do with his diagnosis of a mental disorder.

One method of deciding when a service should be provided by the state is to conduct a cost/benefit analysis. If the alternative to providing therapy is more costly in the long run, there is an argument for state funding. This has been one element in the rationale of the UK's Improving Access to Psychological Therapies (IAPT, n.d.) initiative which is designed to get people off welfare benefits and back into work. This is an attempt to save money while also promoting a form of social welfare that considers it the responsibility of individuals to solve their own problems. It is not clear what policy changes would follow if there turned out to be a net cost in providing therapy. As if to underscore the moral message, the UK disability benefit has been renamed the "personal independence payment". A recent suggestion has been to cut benefits when a recipient refuses to engage in psychological therapy for a "treatable" problem. However, to construe a problem, such as depressed mood, as an easily treated illness is to misconceive the causes of depression and also demonstrates a rather naive faith in brief therapy.

In order to take advantage of IAPT, clients have to be given a psychiatric diagnosis that qualifies them for it. This way of framing the service actually de-emphasises problem-solving and perpetuates the myth that mental illnesses exist. An acceptance of the reality status of illness has led to the suggestion by the main instigators of IAPT that "Schools will routinely measure the well-being of their children, and all teachers will be taught to understand mental illness and how it can be helped" (Layard & Clark, 2014, p. 256). There is an implication here, not directly stated, that any child who is not thriving psychologically is mentally ill.

The widespread adoption of psychiatric criteria has resulted in common problems, such as shyness and grief, being pathologised. In the United States, where many therapists are social workers, Eileen Gambrill, a professor in the field, regards this social trend as dehumanising and as ignoring "decades of experimental research describing the creation of unusual behaviors by unusual learning environments" (Gambrill, 2014). Clearly, if notions of well-being and mental health are allowed to become synonymous, the state can begin to arbitrate on the kind of life we ought to want to lead. An illness label could be applied to anyone who happened to put forward an unacceptable definition of well-being. This is essentially what happened to some dissenters during the Soviet era in Russia. It seems that even the cultivation of happiness can be encouraged for political ends. Yang (2013) argues that the state in China has attempted to pre-empt social unrest by encouraging the poor and the unemployed to engage in psychological self-help in order to unlock their positive potential. Television counselling programmes showcase marginalised people who appear happy despite their limited life circumstances. Expert counsellors glorify role models who have actualised their potential for happiness through becoming entrepreneurs. It seems that politics lies at the very heart of definitions of human suffering.

CHAPTER ELEVEN

Ethics, therapy, and friendship

Throughout this book, I have suggested that therapy shares many of its core values with friendship. Of course, therapy is *not* friendship because it is a service for which a therapist is paid. It is not a voluntary coming together of persons without ulterior motive, a relationship that benefits both parties more or less equally. The website of the British Association of Counsellors and Psychotherapists points out that therapy is *not* "advice giving or persuasion orientated to the therapist's point of view", nor is it "the same as talking with a friend, a parent or sibling, who would probably have an opinion about the issues discussed." Instead, the website emphasises a therapist's impartiality and non-judgemental attitude (BACP, n.d.).

These are clear statements of a professional attitude but the reality of therapy as practised hardly matches up to it. If therapy borrows from the norms of friendship, the boundaries between them are blurred, and this need not be seen as a criticism. In some respects, therapy *is* like talking to a friend. Moreover, it is almost inevitable that a therapist's moral position on the actions a client is contemplating will be detected by a client, however earnestly a therapist attempts to hide them. In most cases, having weighed up the relevant facts, a therapist will have an opinion and would, if invited to do so, offer it. For many clients, this is how they perceive the function of a professional expert. It is true that therapists rarely issue strong directives but a firm opinion is often humbly presented as an impartial assessment of the issues.

Consider, for example, a man who has been repeatedly and inexplicably "dumped" by the same woman in the past year, even though she has acted very lovingly between these times. The man recognises that he has a fear of abandonment relating to childhood events. He wants to renew the relationship with the woman because he is in love with her and he expects her to contact him again. He also expects her to repeat the same painful cycle. His rational mind tells him that to restart the relationship would be an act of masochism but he feels emotionally weak. He looks to the therapist for advice. In my opinion, to refuse to offer advice on grounds of "professionalism" would amount to an excuse for shirking responsibility. The therapist can remain impartial; she does not take the client's side "out of loyalty" and may consider that this particular woman could benefit from therapy as much as the man.

A willingness to offer advice varies a great deal but the codes of conduct that define a professional and ethical relationship with a client are fairly similar across different organisations (Younggren & Gottlieb, 2004). For instance, a therapist does not encourage a client to become a friend, or view his clients as a source of friends when therapy ends. However, this kind of attention to boundaries (as to who and who is not a friend) is also a feature of everyday life. As personal experience should tell, and overheard telephone conversations testify, friends constantly police each other informally through moral judgements of another's behaviour. We comment on friends' gratitude or the lack of it, their honesty or the lack of it, their reliability or the lack of it, and so on. Friends also place limits on self-disclosure and confidentiality. I rather doubt that any person is completely open about themselves with a friend or therapist. Openness with a therapist, who is initially a stranger, may feel safer and easier. Both parties understand the need to respect the privacy of certain disclosures and to keep them confidential. A friend may be less reliable in this respect. It may not be advisable for a client to become a therapist's friend but in some respects a therapist always acts *like* a friend.

I will now discuss a number of ethical issues in greater depth, and show how they are handled in professional codes of practice. It should be made clear that therapists do not deal with their ethical dilemmas in isolation. It is a requirement that a therapist arrange regular meetings with a nominated peer supervisor who provides a forum for discussing these and other practice issues.

Confidentiality

In my experience, clients rarely ask about controls on the confidentiality of the information they divulge but they assume it and of course deserve it (Younggren & Harris, 2008). If they can afford to do so, clients may choose to pay for private therapy because they do not want a public record of their therapy to appear in a medical file. In other words, they do not want a diagnosis or sensitive information to be become "official data", information that could prejudice career advancement, health insurance cover, and possibly other matters where risk is assessed. For instance, one of my clients applying for admission to a postgraduate teaching course was required to complete a form asking about her mental health history. I offered advice about how to complete it in a way that was unlikely to bar her selection. If the university had sought out an official record, the information it contained might well have been prejudicial. This is so because mental ill-health still carries a stigma.

Therapy is commonly funded by a third party, which means that confidential information has to be supplied in order for a service to be provided at all. The third party could be a general practitioner, a hospital clinic, a healthcare provider, or a company handling insurance claims. These records are normally held securely and confidentially but there is always a concern about the hacking of digital data or access by unauthorised personnel. Clients may not know what they have consented to or may feel pressured when allowing confidential data to be passed on (Corcoran & Winslade, 1994).

In the UK National Health Service, it is not permitted to keep private case notes, although there are times when a client will divulge something "in confidence", not wanting it to be written down. Of course, not everything needs to be written down and a good many details are kept in a therapist's head. It is often when a client has the most important things to say that a therapist gives his complete attention and therefore refrains from jotting down notes. It is usual to assign levels of confidentiality to what a client reveals. There is often a requirement to communicate with third parties who have a right to receive information, and this can be done on a "need to know" basis. Before information is passed on, a client is usually asked to scrutinise and approve it.

In rare circumstances, it is a legal requirement to reveal information given in confidence. This may be the case when the client or member of the public needs to be protected from serious harm (e.g., through criminal intent, domestic violence, or terrorism), or when there is abuse or neglect of children and other vulnerable persons. Information may also be requested under a court order. Clients are usually informed of these exceptions to confidentiality at the start of therapy. It has recently been suggested (in the UK) that therapists should be legally required to supply information that has been revealed about sexual abuse. This may be justified if the abuse is ongoing but clients' knowledge that their information will be passed on may inhibit them from revealing it at all, especially if it involves a close family member. This could have the consequence of the client feeling (and actually being) responsible for the break-up of a family and the placement of children in care. In the case of historical child abuse, the argument is far less persuasive for compelling a therapist to make a client's disclosures public. A client might have a great need to come to terms with historical abuse but may not wish to make it the subject of a police investigation. The implications of doing so could be far reaching and have very severe consequences. However, the advantages and disadvantages of going public should, of course, be discussed.

At some point therapy comes to an end, apparently releasing a therapist from his duty of care towards a client. However, a therapist is still in possession of privileged information that a client wishes to keep confidential and so the duty does not end at this point.

The blurred boundary between therapy and friendship

If a therapist is a special kind of friend, this is not a friend with the conventional boundaries of friendship. Any blurring of the social roles of therapist and friend could undermine a number of the advantages that therapy is able to supply. For instance, by socialising with her therapist, a client may worry that confidences could be revealed, wittingly or unwittingly. A therapist's privileged knowledge could also give rise to an ethical dilemma when he becomes aware that a client (or former client) is behaving in a way that is harmful to others within a common friendship circle. This sort of situation is not uncommon between friends as well when, for example, someone has privileged knowledge of a secret liaison. Another reason for preserving a social boundary is a risk that a therapist will no longer be able to judge matters impartially. Decisions could be influenced by factors that have nothing to with the problem for which help is sought. A therapist, out of loyalty to a "friend", could take sides against other interested parties. It is for this reason that therapists rarely offer their services to a relative or personal acquaintance. From the client's perspective, a therapist can no longer be trusted to take an objective view (Younggren & Gottlieb, 2004).

However, there are arguments for and against a rigid enforcement of the boundaries laid out in professional codes of conduct. The usual practice is to see clients in dedicated office surroundings and the service is strictly orientated towards working on an identified problem. However, at times, it may be necessary to employ a technique outside the confines of an office. For a cognitive behavioural therapist, this is routine. For instance, when helping clients, male or female, overcome anxieties associated with public situations, I have accompanied them on all forms of transport, walked in public parks, eaten with them in restaurants, sat with them in pubs, ridden in lifts, and walked along the top of high walls. The purpose in each case was therapeutic, not to cultivate friendship, and as far as I am aware, it was never interpreted as such. By contrast, for some psychodynamic therapists, the surroundings in which they work are designed to be neutral and unchanging, and to give little away about a therapist's private life. Strict attention is given to regular meetings at a fixed time, and elaborate precautions are taken when a therapist is unavailable due to illness or vacations.

Apart from the usual civilities, the extent to which the tone of a therapy relationship takes on a friendly nature can vary enormously. Therapists cannot help revealing their own personality in minor or major ways. They are advised to avoid disclosures about their private life, if only because it is irrelevant to the work in hand. However, reviewing the need for boundaries in psychotherapy, Pope and Keith-Spiegel (2008) show how difficult it is to lay down hard and fast rules. These authors stress how every client, therapist, and situation is unique. For instance, they give the following example: "We help a client take off a winter coat, meaning only to be polite and helpful, unaware that they may experience our stepping too close, touching, and removing an article of clothing as unwanted, intrusive, disrespectful, or even frightening and seductive" (ibid., p. 644).

The rights and wrongs of maintaining an impersonal distance arouses strong debate, as an article by Arnold Lazarus (1994a) and a number of invited replies reveals (Brown, 1994; Gabbard, 1994; Gottlieb, 1994). Lazarus opposes an over-strict interpretation of rules that prohibit contact with a client other than for strictly therapeutic purposes. He feels that a rigid adherence to boundaries can become artificial and backfire by breeding alienation and distance. He offers examples of "human decency" from his own experience, such as inquiring over the telephone about the results of tests concerning a client's medical condition, offering tea and toast to a client who arrives early for an appointment, conducting a session in the more convenient location of a restaurant rather than in an office, playing tennis with a client, and giving and receiving small gifts. He stresses that flexibility should be decided on a case-by-case basis, but he acknowledges that in some instances it is advisable to follow the rules very strictly. He admits that some of his closest friends are ex-clients although he now no longer takes the risks he was prepared to take early on in his career. As a result, he feels that his guardedness about potential malpractice suits has made him a less humane practitioner.

The replies to this article were, in general, hostile. Gabbard (1994) interprets "extensions of humaneness" as attempts to take care of a client's needs like a parent. He also feels one should not confuse "work" and "social" roles. Gottlieb (1994) believes it is never acceptable to stray over strict boundaries. Brown (1994) asserts that there is commonly a failure to appreciate the full extent of a therapist's power and therefore the potential to abuse the trust of a client. She still feels that ethical guidelines should be interpreted flexibly when a therapist confronts a moral dilemma. The same applies when deciding whether malpractice has occurred. She joins with Lazarus in arguing that the present ethical and legal framework is a "concrete, literal-minded, and legalistic one" which "is destructive to the human relational qualities of psychotherapy" (ibid., p.280). Brown would therefore be opposed to a form of professional regulation modelled on the legal system.

In reply to his critics, Lazarus (1994b) reasserts his belief in commonsense flexibility. His position is that therapy stands for a vast array of processes and procedures, so that it is impossible to predict fully the consequences of each and every action. If offence is caused on occasion, this may be explored to reveal new aspects of a client's problem. In a later paper, Zur and Lazarus (2002) distinguish between boundary *crossings* and boundary *violations*, the former defined as benign and beneficial, the latter harmful or exploitative. This inevitably leaves a grey area between them, with retrospective second-guessing when the matter is reviewed after a complaint has been made (Glass, 2003).

Given that it is only rarely necessary to *have* to blur boundaries, as laid out in codes of conduct, it seems sensible on these occasions to review the decision carefully. If concern persists, it can be discussed with a colleague and documented in writing. Once therapy has finished, there are somewhat fewer worries about social contact with a former client. Opinion is divided over whether an ordinary social relationship with a former client creates an ethical problem (Anderson & Kitchener, 1996). There are often pros and cons in each case.

Opinion is less divided over the question of a sexual relationship with a former client. All professional regulators prohibit such relationships during therapy but may not condemn it after a reasonable period of time has elapsed beyond its termination. Others argue that any social contact with a client or former client sets the occasion for a slippery slope into a sexual relationship. In the opinion of some therapists, once a client, always a client. This attitude condemns a client to never achieving parity as a person who is equally responsible for making her own decisions. This is rather like the stigma of a psychiatric diagnosis that can never be erased from the records. Nevertheless, it stands to reason that when a client has become heavily dependent, attached, grateful, or otherwise enmeshed with a therapist, warning bells should sound if contact is continued once therapy has ended. Therapists are advised to proceed with considerable soul-searching before embarking on a sexual relationship with a former client. Although many forms of social contact of a non-romantic kind are quite harmless, a client might see the situation differently, and therefore serious thought needs to be given to this possibility.

Is there a definition of "being in therapy"?

All of the ethical considerations listed above depend on knowing when therapy begins and ends, which is not as simple a matter as it may seem. Ethical guidelines and professional codes of practice seem to carry the presumption that therapy has already been established in a contractual sense. One common-sense definition of the start of therapy would be an agreement to work on a problem in a particular way for a period of time that can be broadly estimated. The ending of an agreement of this type is rarely abrupt because sessions may trail off at longer intervals. A review might be arranged in six months or a year's time, with an understanding that a client can return earlier if so wished.

Professional regulators are more likely to give an unequivocal answer to the definition of a professional relationship with a client, meaning that any kind of contact, however casual, would fall under the same code of conduct. For instance, when a professional title is protected in law (i.e., when using that title without being officially registered constitutes a criminal offence), even a response to an enquiry over the telephone or a letter to another professional, would amount to "professional practice". In other words, a person could claim to be a client and to have been misadvised based on minimal contact. Reasonable persons are unlikely to do so but a litigious person might.

This question of when therapy begins has largely been unexplored, even though its implications are far-reaching. It is important to establish criteria because one would assume that professional regulation would be more stringent in the case of prolonged therapy relationships than with more routine administrative communications. In an empirical investigation using hypothetical scenarios, Smith, Pomerantz, Pettibone, and Segrist (2012) a sample of therapists and students gave their opinion as to whether a professional relationship had been established. Their answers depended on the intensity of contact (telephone or face-face) and its length (five minutes versus one hour). Students were more relaxed than therapists about a therapist making a dating, social, or business contact with a potential client, especially when the contact had been brief. The pattern of opinions also indicated that establishing a professional relationship was not viewed as necessarily implying client status.

In some forms of community mental health work, it could be unfair to apply a strict definition of "client status" or a "professional relationship" because a person with whom a therapist is working may not see herself as in the client role. Voluntary work also has an ambiguous status as therapy. In the case of a professional with a protected title, the same codes of conduct would apply even though the setting lacks a formal structure. The impulse to act with common humanity could be inhibited by realistic worries about false accusations of improper conduct.

In conclusion, different levels of professional practice do not appear to have been established.

Gifts

Therapists frequently receive small gifts when therapy comes to an end. More rarely, they are offered more expensive gifts or gifts while therapy is still in progress (Brown & Trangsrud, 2008; Willingham & Boyle, 2011). Although codes of conduct stress the importance of maintaining professional boundaries, most therapists accept gifts at the end of therapy as a token of a client's appreciation. It is only when gift-giving seems disproportionate or manipulative that it is likely to be refused.

The giving of a gift to a therapist can be viewed as an example of a familiar cultural practice, where refusal would be experienced as hurtful. However, on the whole, solicitors, dentists, pharmacists, etc., do not get offered gifts because the transaction is seen primarily as a commercial transaction rather than a personal one. Willingham and Boyle (2011) interpret gift-giving as a symbolic way of cementing a social relationship, which the anthropologist Marcel Mauss (1925) described as a common phenomenon in cultures across the world. This form of relationship is reciprocal, meaning that givers are takers and vice versa. On this interpretation, therapy could be seen as a gift, in other words, the offer of help or advice is viewed by a client along the same lines as in a friendship, and he may feel an urge to reciprocate. It is important to note that a gift does not have to take a physical form. The very fact that a therapist is willing to listen to a heartfelt tale for long periods at a time, a phenomenon that is rare even amongst friends, makes it into a gift rather than a commercial transaction. A therapist may also "go the extra mile" by finding psycho-educational materials for a client or by supplying small gifts of therapy-related items.

Some therapists might prefer *not* to be seen as a "friend", in which case a gift from a client would be interpreted differently. As some of the psychologists remarked in the study by Willingham and Boyle (2011): "the gift was an attempt to establish himself in control", "difficult for this client to receive help and feel worthy without giving something in return", "trying to penetrate therapeutic boundary" (ibid., p. 177). These interpretations of the gift may have been valid; gift-giving between friends is also subject to a certain level of scrutiny in order to discern underlying motives. I suggest that a strong case can be made that a therapy relationship is necessarily (although by no means entirely) a form of gift-exchange. As in the case of "boundaries", there is a grey area between an acceptance of this fact and an overly defensive interpretation of "correct professional behaviour".

False accusations

Accusations of misconduct are rare. In the US, a legal search revealed only four cases of non-sexual boundary violations between 1995 and 2002 (Miller & Maier, 2002). However, a fear of false accusations is widespread and understandable. If proven, an accusation could spell the end of a lifelong career and financial ruin. Even when it is possible to disprove them, they can have a similar effect because any accusation casts doubt on a therapist's probity and competence, and the allegation may receive widespread publicity in the media. For a profession that depends on trust, any allegation could be damaging.

In the case of people placed in correctional facilities or forensic inpatient hospitals, false accusations and deliberate attempts to derail therapeutic activity are anticipated, and procedures are put in place to mitigate their impact. The residents of these units do not wish to be there and some will attempt to coerce or manipulate staff. They may strike up a romantic relationship or encourage a staff member into an escalating stream of boundary violations. For this reason, staff in the unit run by these authors were carefully selected and then trained to avoid manipulation. "The initial reaction of most staff was disbelief, particularly at the idea that they might become romantically involved with their patients" (ibid., p. 319). Historical examples could, however, be provided.

The point of mentioning these exceptional circumstances is to alert therapists that they will very occasionally encounter a deviously motivated client and will probably be entirely unaware of the fact and therefore unprepared for it. Therapists are also vulnerable to the risk of working with clients who have no intention of harming a therapist until deep-seated fears are awakened when a therapist reaches out with care and love in a way that a client is simply unable to handle. In their own defence, these clients may accuse the therapist of abusive levels of intimacy that may amount to embellished interpretations of what actually transpired or simply to falsehoods (Hedges, 2002). The risk is greatest with therapists who operate with the "Trust me, I can be there for you" approach. Hedges notes that "licensing boards who are seldom familiar with the original record, who have usually not taken the time to hear personal testimony from either party, who have little or no knowledge of how deep transferences operate, … have been unmoved by the false accusation argument … voting often enough instead to discipline and sanction therapists without even the pretense of an open hearing or fair trial" (ibid., p. 496).

Therapists are also vulnerable when, through a sense of humanity, they go beyond the call of duty in meeting the needs of a vulnerable person. One particularly disadvantaged group is runaway and homeless adolescents. As reported by Meade and Slesnick (2002), one in four children in the US from single-parent households and/or households with more than eight persons run away from home. The temptation for a professional to cross boundaries arises for several reasons: the non-traditional (outreach) context of initial contact; the vague and variable specification of legal obligations, especially the need for parental consent; the difficulty of explaining to the adolescent the nature and limits of the help on offer for the purpose of informed consent; unwillingness on the part of the adolescent to make contact with a family that may have abused or ejected her; inability to contact parents and an adolescent's fear of their retribution if contact is made; the very limited nature (or non-existence) of services that could cater to the client's needs; and pressure to intervene when an adolescent's behaviour is putting herself or others at serious risk. In these circumstances, it is more difficult (and possibly undesirable) to adhere to strict professional boundaries.

In brief, professional codes of conduct seem to be designed for transparent transactions between rational and upright adults. The very nature of work with people with psychological problems means that this assumption is not always valid.

Professional regulation

I will begin by briefly examining evidence on the nature and frequency of allegations of therapists' incompetence or unethical behaviour. For some groups of therapists, regulation has been introduced only recently but over the last fifty years it has become tighter for all practitioners. The *laissez-faire* attitudes of the 1960s and '70s no longer prevail. In a survey of licensed counsellors in the United States, complaints were examined between 1994 and 1999 (Neukrug, Milliken & Walden, 2001). The most frequent complaint (24%) was a blurring of boundaries, that is, a "dual relationship" of a non-sexual kind. The next most frequent complaint was incompetence in facilitating a counselling relationship (17%). Seven per cent concerned a sexual relationship with a client, and five per cent a breach of confidentiality. Of all the complaints received, only ten per cent were formally investigated, and in many cases it was considered that no ethical violation had occurred. The authors note that disciplinary action was taken against only 0.17% of all credentialed counsellors.

An audit of complaints to the British Association for Counselling and Psychotherapy between 1996 and 2006 yielded comparable information in a UK setting (Khele, Symons & Wheeler, 2008). The survey excluded the most serious complaints but there were only three of these in the ten-year period. There were sixty-four complaints against individuals in a membership of approximately 16,000 (i.e., 0.4%). It was judged that there was no case to answer in thirty-nine per cent of the complaints. It needs to be borne in mind that forty per cent of all complaints were brought by the organisation's own members rather than by members of the public, suggesting the existence of a high level of professional self-regulation. If we just look at complaints from clients against individual counsellors (i.e., exclude complaints about supervision and training), only fifty per cent of these fifty-six complaints (over ten years) were upheld at adjudication (i.e., two to three per year). Complaints about breaking of boundaries constituted only twelve per cent of the total, although complaints in another category did include sexual exploitation. The authors note that only a minority of complaints emanate from the lay public. They believe that this may indicate an under-reporting of actual incompetence or unethical practice.

There are published data about practitioner psychologists whose title, unlike counsellor or psychotherapist, is protected in law in the UK. In the year 2011 to 2012, in a total of eleven cases that reached the Health and Care Professions Council's (HCPC) stage of a hearing, not one practitioner was struck off, only one was suspended, and six cases were dismissed (Hallam, 2013b). In relation to the total number of registered psychologists, the percentage of sanctioned registrants was 0.03%. It is therefore clear that the proportion of registrants whose allegation was dismissed as unfounded was far greater than this, and these individuals will have been "punished" by the process of investigation itself.

One conclusion that could be drawn from these data is that this form of regulation is sanctioning only a minute number of practitioners who may simply have been "unlucky" enough to have been detected and where, in addition, there was sufficient evidence to pursue a complaint at a public hearing. Alternative methods of regulation may be more efficient and provide greater protection to the public. The HCPC adopts a quasi-judicial procedure in which barristers are employed to question witnesses and argue the prosecution and defence cases. A panel of three people (expert and lay), advised by a lawyer, produces the final adjudication. Although the procedure resembles a criminal trial, the standard of proof is civil, meaning that culpability is decided on the basis of a balance of probabilities. This process might work when the ethical issues are straightforward and the violation of a code is obvious (e.g., a sexual relationship with a client). In practice, this is rarely the case, and the subtleties of the dilemmas that professionals routinely face are unlikely to receive the kind of detailed and impartial consideration they deserve.

In the year 2013 to 2014, there were eighteen allegations about practitioner psychologists that reached the HCPC stage of having a "case to answer" and were therefore considered for putting forward to a hearing (HCPC, 2014). Five were discontinued through lack of evidence and three led to suspensions of registration for health reasons. Five complaints were judged to be "not well founded". One registrant was suspended for rude and insulting behaviour and one was suspended for inadequate clinical skills. In two of the eighteen HCPC allegations, it was claimed that the registrant's relationship with a client was inappropriate. In a total of 19,919 registrants this represents 0.01%.

Given that so few registrants are sanctioned for incompetent or unethical behaviour, this method of regulation hardly ensures that high professional standards are upheld across the profession. The regulator also monitors supervision arrangements and ongoing professional training but this, by itself, is an insufficient guarantee of competence and ethical standards. According to Barlow (2010), five to ten per cent of clients are left in a worse-off state than when they first entered therapy. This may not be due to incompetence, especially if a client is in a deteriorating situation, but one has to assume that there could be a regulatory problem.

The data presented above raise questions about how best to ensure that therapists are competent and ethical. In my view, the meaning of the decisions that practitioners make, or the actions they undertake, can only be appreciated fully when the context in which they occur is thoroughly examined. An adversarial quasi-judicial process does not seem ideally suited for this purpose. Given the subtlety, variety, and uniqueness of each therapy context, complaints against therapists are probably best investigated by a panel of independent peers who are familiar with the dilemmas that often arise. The adjudication of allegations could be made in light of ethical principles rather than inflexible and concretely specified rules of conduct. With broad principles it is possible to take account of the context, even though ethical reasoning can be problematic when principles are in conflict. A fair judgement of misconduct should be possible when the individual circumstances and the constraints operating in each case are carefully examined (McGivern & Fischer, 2012). In practice, only certain kinds of unprofessional behaviour are strictly illegal. The complexities of decision making are usually routinely discussed in meetings between a therapist and her supervisor. An informal type of regulation has been suggested that involves groups of therapists acting in much the same way as friends do when "policing" each other (Heron, 1997; IPN, n.d.). However, unethical behaviour, such as sexual exploitation, is likely to remain undetected unless a client makes a complaint or a colleague becomes suspicious.

Technical treatment or problem-solving: Ethical implications

The metaphors we use when talking about an area of human life structure the way we think about it (Lakoff & Johnson, 1980). I have touched on this in the chapter on the psychodynamic approach where I suggested that theory has been influenced by the metaphor of the mind as a container, with its various contents and levels. What is obvious from various quotations I have used in this book is that authors frequently juggle their thoughts between medical and problem-solving metaphors, and may even do so in the same sentence. The mixture of metaphors is also apparent in my decision to refer to therapy (medical) and client (denoting a service that solves a problem). The title of my book introduces a third analogy: that therapy is modelled on friendship. Although we can be forgiven for mixing our metaphors, one lesson from this book is that certain organising frameworks dominate our thinking and crowd out alternative perspectives.

If we think of therapy in a medical or technical sense, it shapes our expectations of the ethical standards that a provider of this kind of service should adopt. If someone has a "disorder" we expect him to be returned to a state of "order". Ethically, we expect a provider to stand by this promise. Similar, if our vehicle is disordered, we take it to a workshop and expect parts to be replaced, the engine retuned, and where complete restitution is impossible, we want the vehicle to be patched up. This kind of thinking also permeates some models of psychological problems. Depressed mood has been attributed to defective pathways in the brain that can be rectified with a drug or through physical exercise that releases mood-elevating hormones. Therapy for certain fears or obsessional habits also seems to fit this model because we believe that they are the product of a learning process that can be reversed. Retraining and reskilling can be thought of as a patching-up process. The aims of the service can be specified in advance and we feel entitled to complain about false promises or a harmful or ineffective service.

There are powerful motives for therapists to fall in line with this model of restitution. Many are paid by the state or by health insurance companies that assume that mental ill-health consists of disorders that can be rectified. If therapists were to locate themselves outside this health umbrella, funding from these sources might be reduced or disappear. One suggestion is to reserve the term "psychological treatment" for the alleviation of "psychopathology" and "pathophysiology" within a healthcare context, while the term "psychotherapy" would be reserved for procedures designed to enhance personal adjustment and growth outside of healthcare systems (Barlow & Carl, 2011). These authors are concerned that helping clients to work out problems to do with the meaning of life, with failed relationships, or personal growth will "never be reimbursed by health-care dollars" (ibid., p. 908). They argue that psychotherapy should have its own evidence base in a field defined by positive well-being.

These opinions show just how important the terminology of therapy has become. The ethics of treatment designed to restore normal health, and therapy that is geared towards enhancing personal growth, are likely to differ in significant ways. Restoration promises a certain outcome and the onus for delivering it is on the expert. By contrast, a model of personal growth places responsibility fair and square on the client. The therapist becomes a facilitator, adviser, coach, or problem-solver on the sidelines. In my understanding of the relationship, she is a special kind of friend. The ethics of therapy then resemble the norms governing ordinary friendships.

As Halmos points out, therapy "is not restitution. There is no original integrity to which one can return" (1965, p. 152). This is a slight overstatement but, in essence, true. A person can overcome a trauma but not be returned to their pre-traumatised state. The metaphor of growth is an apt one. There is doubt about where that growth can lead, and the client takes a risk and hopes that the endpoint will be better than the starting point. In this perspective, therapy merges at its boundaries with philosophy, religion, the search for a guru, or forming a friendship with someone whose personality and beliefs are completely different from one's own. The professional codes of conduct that I have been discussing in this chapter seem to be modelled on a different set of assumptions. These are, first, on the concept of a therapist as a restorer of health, second, on a relationship with a therapist who is primarily accountable for bringing about change and, third, on the assumption that clients are rational, well-intentioned, and most probably innocent victims when therapy disappoints them. It seems to me that all three assumptions can be questioned.

REFERENCES

Abramson, L. Y., Alloy, L. B., Hogan, M. E., Whitehouse, W. G., Gibb, B. E., Hankin, B. L., & Cornette, M. M. (2000). The hopelessness theory of suicidality. In: T. E. Joiner & M. D. Rudd (Eds.), *Suicide Science: Expanding Boundaries* (pp. 17–32). Boston: Kluwer.

Ackerman, S. J., & Hilsenroth, M. J. (2001). A review of therapist characteristics and techniques negatively impacting on the therapeutic alliance. *Psychotherapy, 38*: 171–185.

Anderson, S., & Brownlie, J. (2011). Build it and they will come? Understanding public views of 'emotions talk' and the talking therapies. *British Journal of Guidance and Counselling, 39*: 53–66.

Anderson, S. K., & Kitchener, K. S. (1996). Nonromantic, nonsexual posttherapy relationships between psychologists and former clients: An exploratory study of critical incidents. *Professional Psychology: Research and Practice, 27*: 59–66.

Aveline, M. (2005). The person of the therapist. *Psychotherapy Research, 15*: 155–164.

Baardseth, T. P., Goldberg, S. B., Pace, B. T., Wislocki, A. P., Frost, N. D., Siddiqui, J. R., Lindemann, A. M., Kivlighan III, D. M., Laska, K. M., Del Re, A. C., Minami, T., & Wampold, B. E. (2013). Cognitive-behavioral therapy versus other therapies: Redux. *Clinical Psychology Review, 33*: 395–405.

Bacon, F. (1920). *Bacon's Essays* (Ed. A. S. West). Cambridge: Cambridge University Press.

BACP (British Association of Counselling and Psychotherapy) (n.d.). www.bacp.co.uk [accessed 12/11/14].

Barlow, D. H. (2010). Negative effects from psychological treatments. *American Psychologist, 65*: 13–19.

Barlow, D. H., Allen, L. B., & Choate, M. L. (2004). Toward a unified treatment for emotional disorders. *Behavior Therapy, 35*: 205–230.

Barlow, D. H., & Carl, J. R. (2011). The future of clinical psychology: Promises, perspectives, and predictions. In: D. H. Barlow & P. E. Nathan (Eds.). *The Oxford Handbook of Clinical Psychology* (pp. 891–911). New York: Oxford University Press.

Bergin, A. E. (1971). The evaluation of therapeutic outcomes. In: A. E. Bergin & S. L. Garfield (Eds.), *Handbook of Psychotherapy and Behavior Change* (pp. 217–270). New York: Wiley.

Berne, E. (1957). *A Layman's Guide to Psychiatry and Psychoanalysis*. New York: Simon and Schuster [reprinted Harmondsworth: Penguin, 1971].

Berne, E. (1964). *Games People Play: The Basic Handbook of Transactional Analysis*. New York: Ballantine.

Blagys, M. D., & Hilsenroth, M. J. (2000). Distinctive features of short-term psychodynamic-interpersonal psychotherapy: A review of the comparative psychotherapy process literature. *Clinical Psychology: Science and Practice, 7*: 167–188.

Bollas, C. (1992). *Being a Character: Psychoanalysis and Self Experience*. London: Routledge.

Boyle, M. (2002). *Schizophrenia: A Scientific Delusion?* (2nd edn) London: Routledge.

British Psychoanalytic Council (n.d.). Code of Ethics. http://www.bpc.org.uk/sites/psychoanalytic-council.org/files/4.1%20Code%20of%20Ethics%20Feb%202011.pdf [accessed 14/07/2015].

Brown, L. S. (1994). Concrete boundaries and the problem of literal-mindedness: A response to Lazarus. *Ethics and Behavior, 4*: 275–281.

Brown, C., & Trangsrud, H. B. (2008). Factors associated with acceptance and decline of client gift giving. *Professional Psychology: Research and Practice, 39*: 505–511.

Castonguay, L. G., & Beutler, L. E. (2006). *Principles of Therapeutic Change that Work*. Oxford: Oxford University Press.

Chambless, D. L., & Ollendick, T. H. (2001). Empirically supported psychological interventions: Controversies and evidence. *Annual Review of Psychology, 52*: 685–716.

Claxton, G. (2005). *The Wayward Mind: An Intimate History of the Unconscious*. London: Abacus.

Corcoran, K., & Winslade, W. J. (1994). Eavesdropping on the 50-minute hour: Managed mental health care and confidentiality. *Behavioral Sciences and the Law, 12*: 351–365.

Davis, J. D., Elliott, R., Davis, M. L., Binns, M., Francis, V. M., Kelman, J. E., & Schröder, T. A. (1987). Development of a taxonomy of therapist difficulties: Initial report. *British Journal of Medical Psychology, 60*: 109–119.

Deutsch, C. J. (1984). Self-reported sources of stress among psychotherapists. *Professional Psychology: Research and Practice, 15*: 833–845.

de Waal, F. (2013). *The Bonobo and the Atheist*. New York: Norton.

Dimidjian, S., & Hollon, S. D. (2010). How would we know if psychotherapy were harmful? *American Psychologist, 65*: 21–33.

Driessen, E., Van, H. L., Don, F. J., Peen, J., Kool, S., Westra, D., Hendriksen, M., Schoevers, R. A., Cuijpers, P., Twisk., J. W. R., & Dekker, J. J. M. (2013). The efficacy of cognitive-behavioral therapy and psychodynamic therapy in the outpatient treatment of major depression: A randomized clinical trial. *American Journal of Psychiatry, 170*: 1041–1050.

Duncan, B. L. (2002). The legacy of Saul Rosenzweig: The profundity of the dodo bird. *Journal of Psychotherapy Integration, 12*: 32–57.

Elchardus, M. (2009). Self-control as social control: The emergence of symbolic society. *Poetics, 37*: 146–161.

Elliott, D. M., & Guy, J. D. (1993). Mental health professionals versus non-mental-health professionals: Childhood trauma and adult functioning. *Professional Psychology: Research and Practice, 24*: 83–90.

Elwood, L. S., Mott, J., Lohr, J. M., & Galovski, T. E. (2011). Secondary trauma symptoms in clinicians: A critical review of the construct, specificity, and implications for trauma-focused treatment. *Clinical Psychology Review, 31*: 25–36.

Erwin, E. (1997). *Philosophy and Psychotherapy*. London: Sage.

Eysenck, H. J. (1985). *Decline and Fall of the Freudian Empire*. Harmondsworth: Viking.

Farber, B. A. (1983). Psychotherapists' perceptions of stressful patient behavior. *Professional Psychology: Research and Practice, 14*: 697–705.

Farrand, P., & Woodford, J. (2013). Impact of support on the effectiveness of written cognitive behavioural self-help: A systematic review and meta-analysis of randomised controlled trials. *Clinical Psychology Review, 33*: 182–195.

Fehr, B., Sprecher, S., & Underwood, L. G. (2008). *The Science of Compassionate Love: Theory, Research, and Applications*. Chichester: Wiley-Blackwell.

Feller, C. P., & Cottone, R. R. (2003). The importance of empathy in the therapeutic alliance. *Journal of Humanistic Counseling, Education and Development, 42*: 53–61.

Fish, J. M. (1996). *Culture and Therapy*. Northvale, NJ: Jason Aaronson.

Fleet, D., & Mintz, R. (2013). Counsellors' perception of client progression when working with clients who intentionally self-harm and the impact such work has on the therapist. *Counselling and Psychotherapy Research, 13*: 44–52.

Fonagy, P. (2001). *Attachment Theory and Psychoanalysis.* New York: Other.

Foucault, M. (1981). *The History of Sexuality: An Introduction.* Harmondsworth: Penguin.

Frank, J. D. (1973). *Persuasion and Healing: A Comparative Study of Psychotherapy* (Rev. edn). Baltimore, MD: Johns Hopkins University Press.

Frank, J. D., & Frank, J. B. (1993). *Persuasion and Healing: A Comparative Study of Psychotherapy* (3rd edn). Baltimore, MD: Johns Hopkins University Press.

Freeman, R. B., & Viney, L. L. (1977). Patients' expectations of the therapist role. *Journal of Community Psychology, 5*: 372–379.

Freud, S. (1894). The justification for detaching from neurasthenia a particular syndrome: The anxiety neurosis. *S. E. 3*: 90–117. London: Hogarth.

Friberg, T. (2009). Burnout: From popular culture to psychiatric diagnosis in Sweden. *Culture, Medicine and Psychiatry, 33*: 538–558.

Furedi, F. (2003). *Therapy Culture.* London: Routledge.

Gabbard, G. O. (1994). Teetering on the precipice: A commentary on Lazarus's "How certain boundaries and ethics diminish therapeutic effectiveness". *Ethics and Behavior, 4*: 283–286.

Gamble, C. (2007). *Origins and Revolutions: Human Identity in Earliest Prehistory.* Cambridge: Cambridge University Press.

Gambrill, E. (2014). The Diagnostic and Statistical Manual of Mental Disorders as a major form of dehumanization in the modern world. *Research on Social Work Practice, 24*: 13–36.

Garrett, T. (1994). Sexual contact between psychotherapists and their patients. In: P. Clarkson & M. Pokorny (Eds.). *Handbook of Psychotherapy* (pp. 431–450). London: Routledge.

Geller, J. D. (2005). Style and its contribution to a patient-specific model of therapeutic technique. *Psychotherapy: Theory, Research, Practice, Training, 42*: 469–482.

Gelso, C. J. (2011). *The Real Relationship in Psychotherapy: The Hidden Foundations of Change.* Washington, DC: American Psychological Association.

Gelso, C. J., & Carter, J. A. (1994). Components of the psychotherapy relationship: Their interaction and unfolding during treatment. *Journal of Counseling Psychology, 41*: 296–306.

Gelso, C. J., Rojas, A. E. P., & Marmarosh, C. (2013). Love and sexuality in the therapeutic relationship. *Journal of Clinical Psychology, 70*: 123–134.

Glass, L. L. (2003). The gray areas of boundary crossings and violations. *American Journal of Psychotherapy, 57*: 429–444.

Goffman, E. (1959). *The Presentation of Self in Everyday Life*. New York: Doubleday.

Goldfried, M. R. (2013). What should we expect from psychotherapy? *Clinical Psychology Review, 33*: 862–869.

Goldfried, M. R., & Davila, J. (2005). The role of relationship and technique in therapeutic change. *Psychotherapy: Theory, Research, Practice, Training, 42*: 421–430.

Gottlieb, M. C. (1994). Ethical decision making, boundaries, and treatment effectiveness: A reprise. *Ethics and Behavior, 4*: 287–293.

Grayling, A. C. (2013). *Friendship*. New Haven, CT: Yale University Press.

Greenberg, L. S. (1994). What is "real" in the relationship? Comment on Gelso and Carter (1994). *Journal of Counseling Psychology, 41*: 307–309.

Hallam, R. S. (2013a). *Individual Case Formulation*. San Diego, CA: Academic.

Hallam, R. S. (2013b). HCPC procedures: A cause for concern. *Clinical Psychology Forum*, No. 251, November. Leicester: British Psychological Society.

Halmos, P. (1965). *The Faith of the Counsellors*. London: Constable.

Haug, T. (2014). Therapeutic alliance and therapist competence as predictors of treatment outcome in manualized cognitive behavioural therapy for social anxiety disorder and panic disorder. Paper read at EABCT, September 2014, The Hague. http://app.eabct.eu/programma_details/516 [accessed 14/07/2015].

Haug, T., Nordgreen, T., Ost, L. G., & Havik, O. E. (2012). Self-help treatment of anxiety disorders: A meta-analysis and meta-regression of effects and potential moderators. *Clinical Psychology Review, 32*: 425–445.

HCPC (Health and Care Professions Council) (2014). *Fitness to Practise Annual Report, 2013–2014*. www.hpc-uk.org [accessed 12/12/2014].

HCPC (2015). *Standards of Conduct, Performance and Ethics*. http://www.hcpc-uk.org/assets/documents/10003B6EStandardsofconduct,performanceandethics.pdf [Accessed, 14/07/2015].

Hedges, L. E. (2002). False accusations: Genesis and prevention. *American Journal of Psychotherapy, 56*: 494–518.

Henkelman, J., & Paulson, B. (2006). The client as expert: Researching hindering experiences in counselling. *Counselling Psychology Quarterly, 19*: 139–150.

Herbst, N., Voderholzer, U., Stelzer, N., Knaevelsrud, C., Hertenstein, E., Schlegl, S., Nissen, C., & Külz, A. K. (2012). The potential of telemental health applications for obsessive–compulsive disorder. *Clinical Psychology Review, 32*: 454–466.

Heron, J. (1997). A self-generating practitioner community. In: R. House & N. Totton (Eds.), *Implausible Professions: Arguments for Pluralism and Autonomy in Psychotherapy and Counselling*. Ross-on-Wye: PCCS.

Hersoug, A. G., Høgland, P., Havik, O., von der Lippe, A., & Monsen, J. (2009). Therapist characteristics influencing the quality of alliance in long-term psychotherapy. *Clinical Psychology and Psychotherapy, 16*: 100–110.

Hill, C. E. (2005). Therapeutic techniques, client involvement, and the therapeutic relationship: Inextricably intertwined in the therapeutic process. *Psychotherapy: Theory, Research, Training, 42*: 431–442.

Ho, F. Y., Chung, K., Yeung, W., Ng, T. H., Kwan, K., Yung, K., & Cheng, S. K. (2014). Self-help cognitive-behavioral therapy for insomnia: A meta-analysis of randomized controlled trials. *Sleep Medicine Reviews, 30*: 1–12.

Hobson, R. F. (1994). *Forms of Feeling: The Heart of Psychotherapy.* London: Routledge.

Hochschild, A. (1983). *The Managed Heart: Commercialization of Human Feeling.* Berkeley, CA: University of California Press.

Holdsworth, E., Bowen, E., Brown, S., & Howat. D. (2014). Client engagement in psychotherapeutic treatment and associations with client characteristics, therapist characteristics, and treatment factors. *Clinical Psychology Review, 34*: 428–450.

Horvath, A. O., Del Re, A. C., Flückiger, C., & Symonds, D. (2011). Alliance in individual psychotherapy. *Psychotherapy, 48*: 9–16.

Hunsley, J., Aubry, T. D., Vestervelt, C. M., & Vito, D. (1999). Comparing therapist and client perspectives on reasons for psychotherapy termination. *Psychotherapy: Theory, Research, Practice, Training, 36*: 380–388.

IAPT (Improving Access to Psychological Therapies) (n.d.). www.iapt.nhs.uk [accessed 12/12/2014].

Illouz, E. (2008). *Saving the Modern Soul: Therapy, Emotions, and the Culture of Self-help.* Berkeley: University of California Press.

IPN (Independent Practitioners Network) (n.d.). www.i-p-n.org. [accessed 12/12/2014].

James, A. (2001). *Raising our Voices: An Account of the Hearing Voices Movement.* Gloucester: Handsell.

Jennings, L., & Skovholt, T. M. (1999). The cognitive, emotional, and relational characteristics of master therapists. *Journal of Counseling Psychology, 46*: 3–11.

Jones, M. C. (1924). Elimination of children's fears. *Journal of Experimental Psychology, 7*: 382–397.

Karon, B. P., & Widener, A. J. (1995). Psychodynamic theories in historical perspective. In: B. Bongar & L. E. Beutler (Eds.), *Comprehensive Textbook of Psychotherapy: Theory and Practice* (pp. 24–47). New York: Oxford University Press.

Khele, S., Symons, C., & Wheeler, S. (2008). An analysis of complaints to the British Association for Counselling and Psychotherapy, 1996–2006. *Counselling and Psychotherapy Research, 8*: 124–132.

Kiropoulos, L. A., Klein, B., Austin, D. W., Gilson, K., Pier, C., Mitchell, J., & Ciechomski, L. (2008). Is internet-based CBT for panic disorder and agoraphobia as effective as face-to-face CBT? *Journal of Anxiety Disorders, 22*: 1273–1284.

Kirsch, I., Lynn, S. J., Vigorito, M., & Miller, R. R. (2004). The role of cognition in classical and operant conditioning. *Journal of Clinical Psychology, 60*: 369–392.

Kraus, D. R., Castonguay, L. G., Boswell, J. F., Nordberg, S. S., & Hayes, J. A. (2011). Therapist effectiveness: Implications for accountability and patient care. *Psychotherapy Research, 21*: 267–276.

Krause, M., Altimir, C., & Horvath, A. (2011). Deconstructing the therapeutic alliance: Reflections on the underlying dimensions of the concept, *Clínica y Salud, 22*: 267–283.

Lakoff, G., & Johnson, M. (1980). *Metaphors We Live By*. Chicago, IL: University of Chicago Press.

Lambert, M. J. (1976). Spontaneous remission in adult neurotic disorders: A revision and summary. *Psychological Bulletin, 83*: 107–119.

Lambert, M. J. (2013). Outcome in psychotherapy: The past and important advances. *Psychotherapy, 50*: 42–51.

Lambert, M. J., & Ogles, B. M. (2004). The efficacy and effectiveness of psychotherapy. In: M. Lambert (Ed.), *Bergin and Garfield's Handbook of Psychotherapy and Behavior Change* (5th edn) (pp. 139–193). New York: Wiley.

La Rochefoucauld, F. duc de, (1959). *Maxims* (Trans. L. Tancock). Harmondsworth: Penguin.

Law, I. (1999). A discursive approach to therapy with men. In: I. Parker (Ed.), *Deconstructing Psychotherapy* (pp. 115–131). London: Sage.

Layard, R., & Clark, D. M. (2014). *Thrive: The Power of Evidence-based Psychological Therapies*. London: Allen Lane.

Lazarus, A. A. (1994a). How certain boundaries and ethics diminish therapeutic effectiveness. *Ethics and Behavior, 4*: 255–261.

Lazarus, A. A. (1994b). The illusion of the therapist's power and the patient's fragility: My rejoinder. *Ethics and Behavior, 4*: 299–306.

Leahy, R. L. (2001). *Overcoming Resistance in Cognitive Therapy*. New York: Guilford Press.

Leeming, D., Boyle, M., & Macdonald, J. (2009). Accounting for psychological problems: How user-friendly are psychosocial formulations. *Clinical Psychology Forum, 200*: 12–17.

Lemma, A. (2014). Off the couch, into the toilet: Exploring the psychic uses of the analysts toilet. *Journal of the American Psychoanalytic Association, 62*: 35–56.

Lemma, A., Roth, A. D., & Pilling, S. (2014). The competences required to deliver effective psychoanalytic/psychodynamic therapy. www.ucl.ac.uk/CORE [accessed 20/05/2014].

Levitt, H. M., & Williams, D. C. (2010). Facilitating client change: Principles based upon the experience of eminent psychotherapists. *Psychotherapy Research, 20*: 337–352.

Lietaer, G. (1992). Helping and hindering processes in client-centered/ experiential psychotherapy: A content analysis of client and therapist post-session perceptions. In: S. G. Toukmanian & D. L. Rennie (Eds.), *Psychotherapy Process Research: Paradigmatic and Narrative Approaches* (pp. 134–162). London: Sage.

Lilienfeld, S. O., Ritschel, L. A., Lynn, S. J., Cautin, R. L., & Latzman, R. D. (2013). Why many clinical psychologists are resistant to evidence-based practice: Root causes and constructive remedies. *Clinical Psychology Review, 33*: 883–90.

Linehan, M. (1993). *Cognitive-behavioral Treatment of Borderline Personality Disorder*. New York: Guilford.

Linley, P. A., & Joseph, S. (2007). Therapy work and therapist's positive and negative well-being. *Journal of Social and Clinical Psychology, 26*: 385–403.

Lomas, P. (1993). *Cultivating Intuition: An Introduction to Psychotherapy*. Northvale, NJ: Jason Aronson.

Loucas, C. E, Fairburn, C. G., Whittington, C., Pennant, M. E, Stockton, S., & Kendall, T. (2014). E-therapy in the treatment and prevention of eating disorders: A systematic review and meta-analysis. *Behaviour, Research & Therapy, 63*: 122–131.

Luborsky, L., Singer, B., & Luborsky, L. (1975). Comparative studies of psychotherapy. *Archives of General Psychiatry, 32*: 995–1008.

Lutz, W., Leon, S. C., Lyons, J. S., Martinovich, Z., & Stiles, W. B. (2007). Therapist effects in outpatient psychotherapy: A three-level growth curve approach. *Journal of Counseling Psychology, 54*: 32–39.

Martin D. J., Garske, J. P., & Davis, K. (2000). Relation of the therapeutic alliance with outcome and other variables: A meta-analytic review. *Journal of Consulting and Clinical Psychology, 68*: 438–450.

Maslach, C., Schaufeli, W. B., & Leiter, M. P. (2001). Job burnout. *Annual Review of Psychology, 52*: 397–422.

Maslow, A. H. (1970). *Motivation and Personality* (2nd edn). New York: Harper and Row.

Masson, J. M. (1988). *Against Therapy: Emotional Tyranny and the Myth of Psychological Healing*. Monroe, ME: Common Courage.

Masson, J. M. (1992). *The Assault on Truth: Freud's Suppression of the Seduction Theory*. New York: Perennial.

Mauss, M. (1925 [1990]). *The Gift: The Form and Reason for Exchange in Archaic Societies* (Trans. W. D. Hall). London: Routledge.

Mayes, R., & Horwitz, A. V. (2005). DSM-III and the revolution in the classification of mental illness. *Journal of the History of Behavioral Science, 41*: 249–267.

McCarthy, W. C., & Frieze, I. H. (1999). Negative aspects of therapy: Client perceptions of therapists' social influence, burnout, and quality of care. *Journal of Social Issues, 55*: 33–50.

McGivern, G., & Fischer, M. D. (2012). Reactivity and reactions to regulatory transparency in medicine, psychotherapy and counselling. *Social Science and Medicine, 74*: 289–296.

McLeod, J. (2010). *Case Study Research in Counselling and Psychotherapy*. London: Sage.

McLeod, J. (2012). What do clients want from therapy? A practice-friendly review of research into client preferences. *European Journal of Psychotherapy and Counselling, 14*: 19–32.

McLeod, J. (2013). Developing pluralistic practice in counselling and psychotherapy: Using what the client knows. *The European Journal of Counselling Psychology, 2*: 51–64.

Meade, M. A., & Slesnick, N. (2002). Ethical considerations for research and treatment with runaway and homeless adolescents. *Journal of Psychology, 136*: 449–463.

Miller, R. B. (2004). *Facing Human Suffering: Psychology and Psychotherapy as Moral Engagement*. Washington, DC: American Psychological Association.

Miller, R. B. (2005). Suffering in psychology: The demoralization of psychotherapeutic practice. *Journal of Psychotherapy Integration, 15*: 299–336.

Miller, R. D., & Maier, G. J. (2002). Nonsexual boundary violations: Sauce for the gander. *Journal of Psychiatry and the Law, 30*: 309–329.

Moloney, P. (2013). *The Therapy Industry: The Irresistible Rise of the Talking Cure, and Why it Doesn't Work*. London: Pluto.

Montaigne, Michel de (1877). *Essays of Michel de Montaigne* (Trans. C. Cotton, Ed. C. Hazlitt). Project Gutenberg. www.gutenberg.org/files/3600/3600-h/3600-h.htm [accessed 21/02/15].

Murphy, D. (2011). Unprecedented times in the professionalisation and state regulation of counselling and psychotherapy: The role of the Higher Education Institute. *British Journal of Guidance & Counselling, 39*: 227–237.

Myrc, J. (1902). *Instructions for Parish Priests*. (Ed. E. Peacock). Early English Text Society, original series, *31*: 1868.

Neukrug, E., Milliken, T., & Walden, S. (2001). Ethical complaints made against credentialed counselors: An updated survey of state licensing boards. *Counselor Education & Supervision, 41*: 57–70.

Nolan, P. (2012). *Therapist and Client: A Relational Approach to Psychotherapy*. Chichester: Wiley-Blackwell.

Norcross, J. C., & Lambert, M. J. (2011). Evidence-based therapy relationships. In: J. C. Norcross (Ed.) Psychotherapeutic Relationships that Work. New York: Oxford University Press.

Norcross, J. C., & Lambert, M. J. (2014). Relationship science and practice in psychotherapy: Closing commentary. *Psychotherapy (Chic.), 51*: 398–403.

Norcross, J. C., & Wampold, B. E. (2011). Evidence-based therapy relationships: Research conclusions and clinical practices. *Psychotherapy, 48*: 98–102.

O'Hara, M. (2009). Who stole psychology and how might humanistic psychologists get it back? *Society for Humanistic Psychology Newsletter,* October, Washington, DC: American Psychological Association.

Okiishi, J., Lambert, M. J., Nielson, S. L., & Ogles, B. M. (2003). Waiting for supershrink: An empirical analysis of therapist effects. *Clinical Psychology and Psychotherapy, 10*: 361–373.

Orlinsky, D. E. (2009). The "generic model of psychotherapy" after 25 years: Evolution of a research-based metatheory. *Journal of Psychotherapy Integration, 19*: 319–339.

Orlinsky, D. E., & Ronnestad, M. H. (2005). *How Psychotherapists Develop: A Study of Therapeutic Work and Professional Growth.* Washington, DC: American Psychological Association.

Pagano, C. J. (2012). Exploring the therapist's use of self: Enactments, improvisation and affect in psychodynamic psychotherapy. *American Journal of Psychotherapy, 66*: 205–226.

Peck, D. F. (2010). The therapist–client relationship, computerized self-help and active therapy ingredients. *Clinical Psychology and Psychotherapy, 17*: 147–153.

Persons, J. B. (2008). *The Case Formulation Approach to Cognitive-behavior Therapy.* New York: Guilford.

Pilgrim, D. (1997). *Psychotherapy and Society.* London: Sage.

Pines, A. M., & Keinan, G. (2005). Stress and burnout: The significant difference. *Personality and Individual Differences, 39*: 625–635.

Piselli, A., Halgin, R. P., & MacEwan, G. H. (2011). What went wrong? Therapists' reflections on their role in premature termination. *Psychotherapy Research, 21*: 400–415.

Pope, K. S., & Keith-Spiegel, P. (2008). A practical approach to boundaries in psychotherapy: Making decisions, bypassing blunders, and mending fences. *Journal of Clinical Psychology, 64*: 638–652.

Pope, K. S., & Vasquez, M. J. T. (2007). *Ethics in Psychotherapy and Counseling: A Practical Guide* (3rd edn.). New York: Wiley.

Prince, M. (1911). The mechanism of recurrent psychopathic states, with special reference to anxiety states. *Journal of Abnormal Psychology, 6*: 135–160.

Prochaska, J. O., & DiClemente, C. C. (1992). The transtheoretical model of change. In: J. C. Norcross & M. R. Goldfried (Eds.), *Handbook of Psychotherapy Integration* (pp. 300–334). New York: Basic.

Pugh, N. E., Hadjistavropoulos, H. D., Klein, B., & Austin, D. W. (2014). A case study illustrating therapist-assisted internet cognitive behavior therapy for depression. *Cognitive and Behavioral Practice*, *21*: 64–77.

Pusch, D., Dobson, K. S., & O'Brien, P. J. (2012). Psychotherapy. In: V. S. Ramachandran (Ed.), *Encyclopedia of Human Behavior* (2nd edn.) (pp. 240–247). Burlington, MA: Academic.

Rachman, S. (2015). The evolution of behaviour therapy and cognitive behaviour therapy. *Behaviour Research and Therapy*, *64*: 1–8.

Rhodes, R. H., Hill, C. E., Thompson, B. J., & Elliott, R. (1994). Client retrospective recall of resolved and unresolved misunderstanding of events. *Journal of Counseling Psychology*, *41*: 473–483.

Richards, D., & Richardson, T. (2012). Computer-based psychological treatments for depression: A systematic review and meta-analysis. *Clinical Psychology Review*, *32*: 329–342.

Richards, D., & Viganó, N. (2013). Online counseling: A narrative and critical review of the literature. *Journal of Clinical Psychology*, *69*: 994–1011.

Richardson, J. D., & Stewart, D. N. (2009). Medieval confession practices and the emergence of modern psychotherapy. *Mental Health, Religion and Culture*, *12*: 473–484.

Riikonen, E., & Vataja, S. (1999). Can (and should) we know how, where and when psychotherapy takes place? In: I. Parker (Ed.), *Deconstructing Psychotherapy* (pp. 115–131). London: Sage.

Ritzer, G. (1993). *The MacDonaldization of Society*. Newbury Park, CA: Pine Forge.

Rogers, C. R. (1980). *A Way of Being*. Boston, MA: Houghton Mifflin.

Rose, N. (1989). *Governing the Soul: The Shaping of the Private Self*. London: Routledge.

Rosenzweig, S. (1936). Some implicit common factors in diverse methods of psychotherapy. *American Journal of Orthopsychiatry*, *6*: 412–415. [Reprinted in *Journal of Psychotherapy Integration*, 2002, *12*: 5–9].

Salter, A. (1952). *Conditioned Reflex Therapy: The Direct Approach to the Reconstruction of Personality*. London: George, Allen, & Unwin.

Samuels, A. (2014). Shadows of the therapy relationship. In: D. Loewenthal & A. Samuels (Eds.), *Relational Psychotherapy, Psychoanalysis, and Counselling* (pp. 184–192). London: Routledge.

Schneider, K. J., & Leitner, L. M. (2002). Humanistic Psychotherapy. In: *Encyclopedia of Psychotherapy (Volume 1)* (pp. 949–957). New York: Academic.

Schwartz, A., & Goldiamond, I. (1975). *Social Casework: A Behavioral Approach*. New York: Columbia University Press.

Seligman, M. E. P. (1995). The effectiveness of psychotherapy: The *Consumer Reports* study. *American Psychologist, 50*: 965–974.

Serretti, A., & Chiesa, A. (2009). Treatment-emergent sexual dysfunction related to antidepressants: A meta-analysis. *Journal of Clinical Psychopharmacology, 29*: 259–266.

Shedler, J. (2010). The efficacy of psychodynamic psychotherapy. *American Psychologist, 65*: 98–109.

Shedler, J., & Westen, D. (2007). The Shedler–Westen assessment procedure (SWAP): Making personality diagnosis clinically meaningful. *Journal of Personality Assessment, 89*: 41–55.

Skinner, B. F. (1973). *Beyond Freedom and Dignity*. London: Jonathan Cape.

Smail, D. (2005). *Power, Interest, and Psychology: The Elements of a Social Materialist Understanding of Distress*. Ross-on-Wye: PCCS.

Smith, J. A., Pomerantz, A. M., Pettibone, J. C., & Segrist, D. J. (2012). When does a professional relationship with a psychologist begin? An empirical investigation. *Ethics & Behavior, 22*: 208–217.

Smith, K. R. (2009). Psychotherapy as applied science or moral praxis: The limitations of empirically supported treatment. *Journal of Theoretical and Philosophical Psychology, 29*: 34–46.

Smith, M. L., Glass, G. V., & Miller, T. I. (1980). *The Benefits of Psychotherapy*. Baltimore, MD: Johns Hopkins University Press.

Sparks, J. A., Duncan, B. L., & Miller, S. D. (2008). Common factors in psychotherapy. In: J. L. Lebow (Ed.), *Twenty-first Century Psychotherapies: Contemporary Approaches to Theory and Practice* (pp. 453–498). New York: Wiley.

Spurling, L., & Dryden, W. (1989). The self and the therapeutic domain. In: W. Dryden & L. Spurling (Eds.), *On Becoming a Psychotherapist* (pp. 191–214). London: Routledge.

Stiles-Shields, C., Kwasny, M. J., Cai, X., & Mohr, D. C. (2014). Therapeutic alliance in face-to-face and telephone-administered cognitive behavioral therapy. *Journal of Consulting and Clinical Psychology, 82*: 349–354.

Sussman, M. B. (2007). *A Curious Calling: Unconscious Motivations for Practicing Psychotherapy* (2nd edn.). Lanham, MD: Jason Aronson.

Swift, J. K., & Greenberg, R. P. (2012). Premature discontinuation in adult psychotherapy: A meta-analysis. *Journal of Consulting and Clinical Psychology, 80*: 547–559.

Swift, J. K., Greenberg, R. P., Whipple, J. L., & Kominiak, N. (2012). Practice recommendations for reducing premature termination in therapy. *Professional Psychology: Research and Practice, 43*: 379–387.

Talbot, F. (2012). Client contact in self-help therapy for anxiety and depression: Necessary but can take a variety of forms. *Behaviour Change, 29*: 63–76.

Totton, N. (2006). *The Politics of Psychotherapy: New Perspectives*. New York: McGraw Hill.

Tracey, T. J. (1991). The structure of control and influence in counseling and psychotherapy: A comparison of several definitions and measures. *Journal of Counseling Psychology, 38*: 265–278.

Trepka, C., Rees, A., Shapiro, D. A., Hardy, G. E., & Barkham, M. (2004). Therapist competence and outcome of cognitive therapy of depression. *Cognitive Therapy and Research, 28*: 143–157.

Twomey, C., O'Reilly, G., Byrne, M., Bury, M., White, A., Kissane, S., McMahon, A., & Clancy, N. (2014). A randomized controlled trial of the computerized CBT programme, MoodGYM, for public mental health service users waiting for interventions. *British Journal of Clinical Psychology, 53*: 433–450.

Viereck, G. S. (1930). Glimpses of the great: Sigmund Freud. In: C. Silvester (Ed.), *The Penguin Book of Interviews* (pp. 263–272), Harmondsworth: Penguin, 1994.

Wachtel, P. (1977). *Psychoanalysis and Behavior Therapy: Toward an Integration*. New York: Basic.

Wallach, M. A., & Wallach, L. (1983). *Psychology's Sanction for Selfishness*. San Francisco, CA: W. H. Freeman.

Wampold, B. E. (2001). *The Great Psychotherapy Debate: Models, Methods, and Findings*, Mahwah, NJ: Lawrence Erlbaum.

Wampold, B. E. (2007). Psychotherapy: The humanistic (and effective) treatment. *American Psychologist, 62*: 857–873.

Wampold, B. E. (2010). *The Basics of Psychotherapy: An Introduction to Theory*. Washington, DC: American Psychological Association.

Wampold, B. E., & Brown, G. S. (2005). Estimating variability in outcomes attributable to therapists: A naturalistic study of outcomes in managed care. *Journal of Consulting and Clinical Psychology, 73*: 914–923.

Warner, C. T. (1986). Anger and similar delusions. In: R. Harré (Ed.), *The Social Construction of Emotions* (pp. 135–166). Oxford: Blackwell.

Webb, B. (1938). *My Apprenticeship (Volume 1)*. Harmondsworth: Penguin.

Webb, C. A., DeRubeis, R. J., & Barber, J. P. (2010). Therapist adherence/competence and treatment outcome: A meta-analytic review. *Journal of Consulting and Clinical Psychology, 78*: 200–211.

Westra, H. A., Aviram, A., Barnes, M., & Angus, L. (2010). Therapy was not what I expected: A preliminary qualitative analysis of concordance between client expectations and experience of cognitive-behavioural therapy. *Psychotherapy Research, 20*: 436–446.

Westra, H. A., Constantino, M. J., Arkowitz, H., & Dozois, D. J. A. (2011). Therapist differences in cognitive-behavioral psychotherapy for generalized anxiety disorder: A pilot study. *Psychotherapy, 48*: 283–292.

Wikipedia (n.d.). George Sylvester Viereck. https://en.wikipedia.org/wiki/George_Sylvester_Viereck [accessed 09/07/2015].

Willingham, B., & Boyle, M. (2011). "Not a neutral event": Clinical psychologists' experiences of gifts in therapeutic relationships. *Psychology and Psychotherapy: Theory, Research and Practice, 84*: 170–183.

Wilson, N. (2003). Commercializing mental health issues: Entertainment, advertising and psychological advice. In: S. O. Lilienfeld, S. J. Lynn, & J. M. Lohr, (Eds.), *Science and Pseudoscience in Clinical Psychology* (pp. 425–460). New York: Guilford.

Yang, J. (2013). "Fake happiness": Counseling, potentiality, and psycho-politics in China. *Ethos, 41*: 292–312.

Young, J. E., Klosko, J. S., & Weishaar, M. (2003). *Schema Therapy: A Practitioner's Guide*. New York: Guilford.

Younggren, J. N., & Gottlieb, M. C. (2004). Managing risk when contemplating multiple relationships. *Professional Psychology: Research and Practice, 35*: 255–260.

Younggren, J. N., & Harris, E. A. (2008). Can you keep a secret? Confidentiality in psychotherapy. *Journal of Clinical Psychology in Session, 64*: 589–600.

Zapf, D., Vogt, C., Seifert, C., Mertini, H., & Isic, A. (1999). Emotion work as a source of stress: The concept and development of an instrument. *European Journal of Work and Organizational Psychology, 8*: 371–400.

Zeeck, A., Orlinsky, D. E., Hermann, S., Joos, A., Wirsching, M., Weidmann, W., & Hartmann, A. (2012). Stressful involvement in psychotherapeutic work: Therapist, client and process correlates. *Psychotherapy Research, 22*: 543–555.

Zur, O., & Lazarus, A. (2002). Six arguments against dual relationships and their rebuttals. In: A. Lazarus & O. Zur (Eds.), *Dual Relationships and Psychotherapy* (pp. 3–24). New York: Springer.

INDEX

For Product Safety Concerns and Information please contact our EU
representative GPSR@taylorandfrancis.com
Taylor & Francis Verlag GmbH, Kaufingerstraße 24, 80331 München, Germany

www.ingramcontent.com/pod-product-compliance
Lightning Source LLC
LaVergne TN
LVHW021128300926
849160LV00010B/917

9781782202523